A Six-Pack and a Fake I.D.

TEENS LOOK AT THE DRINKING QUESTION

BY SUSAN AND DANIEL COHEN

M. Evans and Company, Inc.   New York

The poem by Ogden Nash that is quoted in Chapter 6 is from *Verses from 1929* by Ogden Nash. Copyright 1930 by Ogden Nash. First appeared in *The New Yorker*. Reprinted by permission of Little, Brown and Co. (Inc.).

Library of Congress Cataloging-in-Publication Data

Cohen, Susan.
 A six-pack and a fake I.D.

  Bibliography: p.
  Includes index.
  Summary: Discusses the role of drinking in our society, the various reasons people drink, the physiological effects of alcoholic beverages, popular misconceptions about alcohol, the differences between drunkenness and alcoholism, and other aspects of the issue about which teenagers need to make an informed decision.
  1. Youth—United States—Alcohol use—Juvenile literature. [1. Alcohol] I. Cohen, Daniel. II. Title.
HV 5135.C64   1986   362.2'92   85-25337

ISBN 0-87131-459-2

M. Evans and Company, Inc.
216 East 49 Street
New York, New York 10017

Design by Lauren Dong

Manufactured in the United States of America

9 8 7 6 5 4

Contents

How to Get into Harvard

Drinking—it's a fact of life that you confront in your teen years. You may consider drinking a pleasure, a right, and a social necessity. Your parents, your school, and the over-twenty-one world in general may consider your drinking a problem—and they have made it illegal to boot. But you're not going to let that stop you!

It's Presidents' Weekend, vacation time, and you need it. Your bus pulls into the Port Authority Bus Terminal about noon, and you nudge your friend Steve to wake him up. You're in for a day in New York City, and last night you stayed up until 4:00 AM planning what you'd do. You've got twofers for a musical. Maybe you'll try ice skating at Rockefeller Center. Or maybe you'll roam around Macy's for a while.

But the big thing you've taken a three-hour bus ride for is to pick up a fake I.D. You're a senior in high school, and though you've tried your best to look older, you don't. At the most, you might pass as a freshman in college. No point kidding yourself. You look and are seventeen in a state where you can't drink legally until you're twenty-one.

Still, back home all your friends said it didn't matter. It isn't hard to get a fake I.D. Then you can walk into any bar where you're not known and get a drink. Oh, they don't have to serve you. A girl you know went into a bar and the bartender took her fake I.D. away from her, told her she was too young, and kicked her out. But not everybody has bad luck.

By now the bus has arrived. Steve is so excited he's getting a little crazy, and the two of you take the escalator down to the street level. Outside the bus station it's crowded. Some of the people look pretty weird, and as you walk around, you notice some of the stores are pretty weird too. But you don't mind. That's part of what makes New York exciting.

A couple of the places you pass have signs posted in the window saying "photo identification." A glance into the window shows you that a lot of teenagers have come to New York to celebrate the long weekend. Only an idiot couldn't spot that they're in the stores buying fake I.D.s. So why delay another minute? You and Steve pick a store at random and go in. Sure, selling fake I.D.s is illegal, but this is Times Square in Manhattan, and anything goes.

The place is jammed with kids. On the walls there are driver's licenses, birth and death certificates, passports and thousands of fake I.D.s. They're cheap, too—under ten bucks. There are I.D.s for just about every college you've ever heard of. Steve says maybe you should pick Harvard. It's as close as you'll get to the Ivy League with your SAT scores. You tell him he'd better forget about an I.D. from Columbia. One look at him and anybody can tell he's from New Jersey. The other teens standing near you laugh, but they're joking around, too. There's an electric excitement about being in the place, and everybody's having fun.

Everybody, that is, except the nasty, fat old guy selling the I.D.s. Despite all the business, he doesn't seem very happy that the small shop is full of teenagers. When you try to buy a Harvard I.D., he tells you he's only selling New York University I.D.s today because he's so busy. He rushes you to pick out a phony name.

Steve calls himself Bill Jones. You think of trying something funny, call yourself Liu Chan or Reggie Jackson or Alex Van Halen, but that would be dumb. You want to use your I.D., so you pick a nice neutral name, Harry Roberts, and you decide to give your real Social Security number and real home address. The main thing is that your birth date on the I.D. shows that you're twenty-one.

Then the grouchy fat guy puts you in a chair and takes your picture. He makes you leave the store for twenty minutes or so while he makes up the I.D. You're a little nervous leaving the store, but nobody pays any attention to you. Nobody seems to care. There are no cops around. Not that you're sure they'd stop you if they were. Getting a fake I.D. around here is just business as usual, ordinary stuff. With all the signs in the window, what's going on is certainly no secret. It's not at all like getting a phony passport in the spy movies. It's so easy it's almost disappointing.

When the time's up, you come back to the store. You look around at the crowd again. Some of the kids seem as young as fifteen.

Armed with your fake I.D., you head for a bar. You and Steve enter coolly, trying to act calm, ready to show the bartender your new I.D. as soon as you order. But he doesn't bother to ask you for it. He just serves you a drink. Still, you and Steve do use your I.D.s later in the day in a liquor store. Other kids are doing the same, and a lot of them look younger than you do. But the guy behind the counter doesn't dispute the I.D.

It's spring break in Freeport, Bahamas. You slip into your bikini and head out to the hotel pool to get some sun. Besides wanting to get a good tan, you need to rest. Last night was wild. This is the first place you've been in your life where there's no minimum drinking age at all.

When you got off the plane yesterday and arrived at the hotel, the first thing you saw was a group of kids, juniors in high school like yourself, carrying what looked like huge crates of beer. And just about everybody from college students on down was walking around with an open beer can or some sort of rum drink. Last night you walked into a bar and ordered a Bahama Mama, a sweet red drink loaded with rum. Nobody batted an eye over your being sixteen. Definitely not like home.

The island is bursting with teens, and although a lot of them are with their parents, who set rules about what time they have to be in at night, most just wait until their parents are asleep and then slip away to the all-night parties. Last night you and your friends pooled your money and went to a disco. At first you were scared nobody would notice you and there was a lot of tension.

It was packed with gorgeous guys, and as everybody relaxed and got drunk you were invited to three parties. John's room was full of kids when you arrived, and the place was such a mess John said the maid refused to clean it anymore. People were sitting on the bed, the floor, the arms of chairs, listening to rock on John's box and drinking. Beer cans and glasses covered every inch of space on the dresser and tables, and somebody figured it was funny to line them up on top of the headboard against the wall.

A boy you'd danced with at the disco, Tom, showed up. Though there was a lot of talk about making out, nothing much was happening besides drinking. Some people talked about how somebody had tried to sell them grass and cocaine when they were out shopping, but nobody wanted it. When a couple of kids began smoking regular cigarettes John told them he thought smoking was a dangerous, crazy thing to do. He wouldn't smoke.

The beer was running low, and one guy bragged that he'd already had two six-packs, but that was nothing for him. He was ready for more. Two boys went down in the elevator to the bar and came back with a basin filled with ice water and loaded with bottles of beer.

An hour later you felt like everybody was your best friend. People had their arms wrapped around each other and were swaying and singing. The boy next to you was telling you crazy wild stories about last spring break when he was in Fort Lauderdale. The beach and ocean are on one side of the strip, bars and hotels on the other.

He told you about the nightclubs that advertise fake I.D. nights, mud wrestling, wet nightgown contests, and how once you hit the strip at night there's a huge traffic jam and people jump into and onto cars. It's a twenty-four-hour-a-day party and the beer just flows. While he talked you were thinking about what a great story the party will make when you get back home, and you started giggling and couldn't stop.

It was a fantastic game. Basketball is a religion at your school, and you were part of the crowd that saw your team beat its closest rival, taking the conference championship. It was pure pandemonium with everybody screaming and yelling when the final buzzer went off. It was a moment you're sure you'll remember the rest of your life.

You got swept up in all the excitement, and after a quick pizza you hit the party circuit. You had your first beer at five, and by nine o'clock you didn't even know whose house you were at. Normally you don't drink much. Track is your big sport and you run even in the winter. Some kids think you're goofy on the subject of health, but you have a crack at a state championship, and that usually means a college scholarship too, so you watch what you eat, keep your weight down, stay in shape.

But tonight is different, special. For a while the drinking was fun. You didn't feel shy, the way you usually do. Everything seemed hilariously funny. When Gary took off his pants and danced around in his underwear you laughed so hard you fell on the floor. But that was a couple of hours ago. By now all the chugalugging has caught up with you. You feel dizzy, queasy, and suddenly you're rushing to the bathroom. You throw up, but you still feel awful.

After you get out of the bathroom you stand with your back against the wall. Somebody floats up to you—you're not seeing things too clearly—and tells you that you look awfully pale. You make a break for the bathroom again, but you don't reach it in time. Now you're sick right on the rug.

Friends come over to help you. You feel stupid and embarrassed but most of all sick. You haven't felt like this since you had a bout of stomach flu. You promise yourself that if you get over this you'll never get drunk again. You collapse on the couch, and people make jokes about how you look like a corpse. You're afraid to go home because your parents will scream and threaten, and you're too weak to take it. Besides, you're not very happy at the thought of having your mother clean up after you.

Somehow your friends bundle you into a car. They toss a coin to see who will get stuck with you tonight. Somebody calls up and lies for you, telling your parents that since it's an icy night they don't want to drive you home. Can you stay?

You spend most of the night curled up on the bathroom floor, miserable, wondering about what your friend's parents are thinking and what your own parents will say tomorrow and basically wishing you were dead. You fall asleep sometime near dawn, wake up with the dry heaves, and get driven home, where your father lectures you and your kid brother makes fun of you. You try everything from cold showers to hot coffee, but you only start to feel vaguely human by nightfall.

Still, for all your promises, one month later you're at another party, and the first thing you do is reach for a beer. Only this time you sip it slowly, grab a handful of peanuts, and tell yourself you'll know when to stop. You get through the night without getting sick. When you wake up the next morning, you don't feel great, but you don't feel terrible either.

Do any of those stories sound familiar to you? They should. They are all true, and they have all happened within the last few months. There is nothing unusual or bizarre about any of these experiences. That's why we chose them.

This is a book about drinking and teens. Please note that *we* did not say this is a book about the "problem" of teenage drinking, for while there can be very severe problems when teens, or anyone for that matter, drink, drinking is not only a problem. For most people in America drinking is an ordinary part of everyday life.

The subject of teens and drinking is certainly not a new one. You've probably talked, even argued about it with your parents. It's been discussed in school, in church, and in community groups. You've heard a lot about it on television. And you've probably been given books and pamphlets to read. Most of all you've talked about drinking with your friends. What can we possibly say about the subject that's new, that you haven't already heard?

In doing research for this book, we've read an awful lot of material about drinking that was written for teens. We had to read the books and pamphlets that are aimed at you. After a while we began to get the feeling that most of the material was written by beings from another planet who had a very warped and one-sided view of life on earth today. They were people writing about the world as they thought it should be, not as it really is.

The overall impression that we got in reading about teens and drinking is that the inevitable result of a few beers at the age of fifteen is a life of degradation and an early death—prostitution and cirrhosis of the liver. Or maybe if you're really lucky, you'll only have to spend the rest of your life in a wheelchair after drunkenly smashing your stolen car into a tree.

But we know that picture is not true or complete—and you know it too. We're going to try to talk about the subject honestly and realistically—no scare stories, no bull.

Maybe you've heard that line before. The writers all sound friendly, reasonable, and understanding, but it's a front because pretty soon you get the prostitution, the cirrhosis, and the wheelchair. We have no hidden message.

The fact is that we drink. And that is not the anguished cry of a couple of alcoholics but a simple statement of fact. Like most Americans we have a drink now and then, and sometimes more than one or more than now and then. We do not see moderate drinking as a problem; indeed, it is often a positive pleasure. Yes, we know people whose lives have been and are being ruined by drinking. Alcoholism is a serious problem in the United States. We also know people—mostly young—who have been killed or seriously injured in drunken driving accidents. This too is part of the story and cannot be ignored. For us, drinking itself is not a moral issue. Drinking too much or at the wrong time presents a host of practical problems that require practical responses.

As a species we might be better off if plant juices didn't ferment and produce the drinkable, intoxicating substance that we call alcohol. It might be nice if the strongest thing that we ever drank were iced tea. But that's not the way it is. We live in a drinking society, and while we Americans are not the biggest drinkers in the world (though we once were), we are not the most abstemious of folk either. If preaching, threatening, and passing laws could stop us from drinking, then we would all have abandoned alcohol long ago, because there has been plenty of preaching, threatening, and lots of laws, yet we Americans still drink.

We both drank as teenagers, even though it was illegal to do so, just as most other teenagers did then, and do now. In school we were shown antidrinking films every bit as silly as *Reefer Madness*. We laughed at them and ignored their message. And we grew up without suffering any serious consequences, just as most of our teenage drinking companions did.

But we also had a lot of misconceptions about drinking—how it affected the body and mind, what the laws were and why they existed, what a hangover was and how to cure it, etcetera. There was a lot of mythology surrounding drinking, and there still is. For many people drinking can be an emotional subject. It can also be a confusing one, for though drinking and all its ramifications have been intensively studied by scientists for a long time, there is still a great deal of honest disagreement, and much remains unknown. We'll try to make the subject as clear as we can.

If you're a fairly average kid, then you probably tasted some sort of alcoholic beverage by the time you were thirteen. By the time you were sixteen, you probably had some drinks at a party—maybe lots of drinks at lots of parties. So we will assume drinking is already a part of your life or soon will be and we think it's a good idea for you to know something about how it affects you physically, mentally, and socially. Even if you don't drink now and never intend to, it's not a bad idea to know about it, because a lot of people around you are going to pressure you to join in. You may have good solid reasons for not drinking.

Drinking, particularly teen drinking, is a very hot topic, now more than ever. We'll also discuss why there is a sudden move to take away a right that many of you had just a few years ago. That too is something you should understand.

Ultimately you are the one who will make the decisions about drinking. We're going to try to provide you with reliable and believable information that will help you make the decisions responsibly.

2

The First Time

Sometimes you're alone when it happens. Usually you're with a crowd. Occasionally you decide in advance to make it happen, but most of the time it just sneaks up on you. "It" is getting drunk for the very first time.

TAMMY

Tammy, fifteen, had never gone in for drinking at parties before, but then she'd always had Ken with her. Just being around her boyfriend, Ken, was special, so special that she could get through even a dull party on a couple of sodas as long as he was there. But two weeks ago she and Ken had a terrible fight. Tammy threw Ken's class ring at him. It hit the floor. Ken reached down, scooped it up, and the next thing Tammy knew he'd stormed out of the house. Now he was going with Judy. Judy, Tammy's worst enemy!

Tammy had half hoped Ken would be here tonight. She still loved him, she still missed him, and she wanted more than anything to make up. Instead, this big dummy Roger, who had liked her since eighth grade, kept pestering her. Tammy signaled her friend Louise to come over and rescue her, but Louise chose not to notice. Too busy chatting with Jim.

Suddenly Tammy couldn't stand it anymore. Roger, drinking like crazy and telling her silly jokes just to get her to notice him; the gloomy January night with the snow falling; Ken's not being there. She had to do something to relieve her emotions, so angrily and defiantly Tammy gulped down a glass of cola laced with vodka.

She began feeling better fast. This encouraged her to have another drink. Okay, this was more like it; this was a party. Not only was Tammy cheerful now, but the mirror showed her that her winter paleness was gone. Well, she felt warm, a nice glowing warm, so of course she looked a little flushed.

She didn't need Louise to rescue her any longer. She felt quite bold enough to join Sandra, Eileen, and Rick, who were having a quiet conversation by themselves. Normally Tammy wouldn't dream of interrupting them because they weren't close friends, but her normal inhibitions were fading fast. Before she could move, there was Roger again, blocking her. He was six feet tall and not exactly what you'd call thin, and she was five feet one and only a hundred pounds. It wasn't easy for Tammy to ignore him. The more she listened to him brag about how much and how fast he could drink, the madder she got. She'd show him. Tammy downed another drink.

She was on the verge of telling Roger off when she was practically knocked off her feet by Louise bolting past her en route to the bathroom. As usual, one stiff drink was enough to do Louise in. Everybody, including Tammy, laughed. Nobody meant to be cruel, but it was ridiculous how Louise threw up at every party.

Tammy realized her laughter sounded awfully loud when a lot of people turned to stare. Usually she was a quiet person. Not only was her voice loud, but her speech was slurred. She kept jumping from subject to subject, starting one story, then forgetting what she was saying and starting another, not finishing that either. Someone told her to slow down, but she ignored the advice and went right on drinking.

Then she started feeling strange. She was sure the party was still noisy, but everything sounded muffled. People seemed to be far away. She couldn't see them clearly, couldn't focus. Not that she felt depressed or tired. Quite the contrary. When someone handed her a piece of cake, she decided it would be hilariously funny to throw it at Roger. He glared and in return pelted her with popcorn. A food fight! She hadn't been in one since seventh grade, and she was having so much fun that she hit Roger in the face with a spoonful of icing. Before he could retaliate, she rushed to the bathroom, for the umpteenth time. She'd never had to pee so often in her life.

On her way back to start up another food fight, Louise grabbed her and told her to keep her hands off the cake. This made Tammy lose her temper, and when she started to yell, her breath smelled so sour Louise reared back.

Tammy heard the people around her saying in concern, "Is Tammy drunk? Tammy, are you all right? Can you sneak past your parents when you get home?" Questions like this seemed stupid, so Tammy made an effort to walk away, but she stumbled and fell. She couldn't get up. It was impossible. The room was spinning. Then Sandra and Eileen took hold of her, dragged her to her feet, and hauled her off to the bathroom. They combed her hair, made her rinse her mouth with mouthwash, forced her to drink black coffee, wrapped her in her coat, and with Rick's help got her to Rick's car.

When the car began to move, Tammy, who was sandwiched between Sandra and Eileen, threw up on both of them. Sandra screamed and Eileen grabbed a handful of tissue, but it was impossible to clean up the mess easily. When Rick pulled up in front of Tammy's house, the lights were on downstairs. That meant Tammy's parents were awake and waiting up for her.

"You've got to go in by yourself," said Eileen. "If we carry you in, they'll know you've been drinking." So Tammy got out of the car by herself and promptly fell face first into a snowbank. Sandra giggled nervously, and Rick got out and brought Tammy up to the house, then turned and fled. The car shot away the minute Tammy's father opened the door.

With her parents yelling at her, threatening her with everything this side of torture for coming home drunk, Tammy staggered to the bathroom. Her mother stripped off Tammy's clothes and threw them in the washing machine while Tammy took a bath. Her mother returned, put Tammy in pajamas, and led Tammy past her kid sister who could hardly be expected to sleep through all the fuss and was being obnoxious and disgustingly sarcastic.

So Tammy was left alone on her bed in the dark where she promptly collapsed. Near dawn she woke up, wondering how she'd gotten to bed. The party was a total blank; she couldn't remember a thing. She went back to sleep. When she opened her eyes hours later, her head ached fiercely. She was dead tired. And she was violently thirsty. Oh, if only she'd spent last night drinking Dr. Pepper!

Tammy's story is classic, as you well know if you've ever been drunk. But you probably know it even if you haven't been, because by the time you're a teenager you know what drunken behavior looks like. You've probably seen friends and relatives get drunk. You've seen drunks in movies and on television. Even little kids know the signs and symptoms. They've watched cartoon characters fall down, talk incoherently, and wobble when they walk, acting drunk. And comedians, of course, tell a lot of jokes about drunks. Unlike, say, heroin or cocaine or even pot, which are usually considered grimly serious business, alcohol strikes most people as having a funny side.

GETTING DRUNK

We talk a lot about getting drunk. Expressions like "stinking drunk," "dead drunk," and "bombed out of his mind" are very common. But, despite the jokes, the first-hand knowledge, the people you meet gulping away at parties, do you know what the word *drunk* really means? Why does alcohol do weird things to your body? How does the process of getting drunk work? There's an expert at every party who thinks he or she knows all about the subject, but by and large people aren't very clear on the details. Your average expert usually has a great deal of misinformation.

Let's start with one basic fact. When we say *alcohol*, we mean ethyl alcohol. All alcohol is toxic, which means poisonous, but ethyl alcohol passes through the body quickly and is the major chemical in distilled liquor, wine, and beer. Don't let that word *toxic* panic you. Every day we take in substances such as caffeine, aspirin, and vitamin A, which are toxic and can be dangerous to health if taken in massive quantity. Imbibing liquor is not like eating poisonous mushrooms. It's only fatal in extreme cases. Methyl alcohol, on the other hand, is *highly toxic* and *should never be drunk*. It is used as an antifreeze in automobile radiators and as a rocket fuel. Occasionally alcoholics will drink it out of desperation, usually with very grim results.

Having made the distinction, we'll simply say alcohol from now on, meaning ethyl alcohol. It's shorter and easier. Alcohol is colorless and highly flammable and has a burning taste. Made up of the chemicals carbon, hydrogen, and oxygen, its formula (if such things interest you) is C_2H_5OH.

Among common beverages, beer and ale contain the lowest percentages of alcohol, usually 4 percent to 5 percent. Wine generally runs from 10 percent to 14 percent alcohol. Fortified wines like port and sherry (*fortified* means extra alcohol has been added) reach 17 percent to 20 percent. Distilled liquor—that's gin, scotch, rum, vodka, the so-called hard liquors—ranges from 40 percent to 70 percent alcohol.

You can learn the alcohol content of a bottle of hard liquor by reading the proof number on the label. The amount of alcohol will be one-half the proof listed. For examples, 86 proof means 43 percent alcohol. And 100 proof vodka is 50 percent alcohol, which is what Tammy was drinking at her party. No wonder she was hard hit!

Although alcohol has little nutritional value, it does have calories, around 125 in an ounce and a half of whiskey. But unlike food, it isn't digested, that is, altered and then brought to cells and tissues via blood plasma. So what happens when you raise your glass and take your first swallow? Approximately 20 percent of the alcohol in your drink will go directly through the stomach walls into your bloodstream, at which point (since it's toxic) your body will start to eliminate it. Alcohol that does not pass directly into the bloodstream goes through the intestines and then enters the bloodstream, a slower process.

Through a series of complicated steps the body eventually changes alcohol to carbon dioxide and water, allowing you to burn off (metabolize) the alcohol. The name of this process is oxidation, and enzymes vital to it are produced in the liver. Your liver sometimes becomes swollen and irritated when you get drunk, but that's only temporary. However, people who drink excessively for years can seriously damage their liver. You've probably heard of cirrhosis of the liver, a fatal disease that often afflicts alcoholics.

Okay, by now you may have figured out that getting drunk is the result of overloading your system with more alcohol than it can metabolize efficiently. How does the body then eliminate alcohol? Let's take a look at our "classic case," Tammy at the party last night. Remember how Louise reeled back at the smell of Tammy's breath? "Whiskey breath" is really alcohol evaporating as one breathes out. Some alcohol, therefore, is eliminated through the lungs.

Perspiration also helps the body get rid of alcohol. So some alcohol is secreted through the sweat glands. Some alcohol passes out unchanged in urine. Tammy spent a good part of the evening dashing to the john. Part of this was due to taking in a lot of liquid, but alcohol affects the pituitary gland in the head, and the pituitary gland helps control how often you must urinate. But a lot of alcohol remains, at least temporarily, in the bloodstream.

Size is a factor in the rate at which alcohol enters the bloodstream and the speed at which it reaches the brain. Tammy is small and thin. No way she could outdrink Roger who's big and heavyset. Roger has more water in his system to dilute alcohol. A word of warning, though. Obese people can get drunk as quickly as thin people because fatty tissue has a low water content. Though tall, broadly built muscular types have an edge when it comes to "holding their liquor," if they drink enough, they too will get drunk.

Of course, there are factors that are hard to measure. Individuals react to alcohol in different ways. Take Louise, who gets sick whenever she drinks. In some cases, alcohol irritates the pyloric valve (located between the stomach and the small intestine), closing the valve and concentrating the alcohol in the stomach. This makes the valve go into spasms. You become nauseated and throw up. Getting sick every time you drink a small amount of alcohol is no fun, but it does give you a built-in system of protection against getting drunk.

The mood you're in when you drink also helps determine whether you get drunk. Tammy started the party in an anxious, tense frame of mind because she missed Ken, and she drank defiantly as a way of releasing tension. Because alcohol acts very quickly on the brain, Tammy's mood changed as she drank and she became cheerful, at least temporarily. Contributing to this feeling of well-being was a sense of warmth. Though alcohol does warm the skin, it doesn't really heat your body. As the skin is warmed, other organs actually lose heat.

This warm happy phase is what many people enjoy about drinking. It makes them feel sociable and relaxed. In general, you reach this stage after two or three beers, a couple of glasses of wine, or a cocktail or two, provided that each cocktail has only one shot glass or jigger's worth of liquor; that would be a single ounce. (A beer, a glass of wine, and an average mixed drink all have about the same amount of alcohol—one-half ounce.) At this point the concentration of alcohol in your bloodstream would be about five hundredths of 1 percent or less (0.05 percent).

It takes about an hour for your body to burn off the amount of alcohol in a single drink (the beer, the wine, or the cocktail), and if Tammy had known that, she could have prevented the buildup of alcohol in her blood. Alas for poor old Tammy—she went right on guzzling away past the tranquilizing stage of drinking, not realizing that alcohol is really a depressant—it slows down brain activity—and that the cheerful stage is temporary.

Because alcohol affects the cells in the outer layer, or cortex, of the brain, as you continue drinking, alcohol alters the way you think and move. By 0.10 percent, speech is slurred. By 0.15 percent, Tammy was having trouble walking. By 0.30 percent, she was throwing up on her friends in the car, and was totally confused and unaware of what was happening to her. At 0.40 percent, people often pass out, which may be just as well, because with a concentration between 0.40 and 0.70 percent you can die. You can also die if you gulp down a pint of liquor on the spot. This is not said to scare you. Just as the ordinary adult isn't likely to drink antifreeze, he or she isn't likely to reach the stage where there's 0.40 percent alcohol in his or her bloodstream either. It's just something you should know.

So now you see what getting drunk is. The next stage in the process is also notorious; the hangover. As Tammy, lying in a dark bedroom, thirsty, exhausted, and assailed by a ferocious headache, would tell you herself, it's the pits.

3

"I Think I'm Going to Die"

Can you relate to this? Last night was fun. At least the first part of the evening was fun. The whole crowd was there. Everybody was having a good time. You had been feeling a little nervous about the party, so you had a couple of quick drinks, just to relax a bit—and they did the trick. You not only felt comfortable, you were really witty. People laughed at your jokes. And you laughed at other people's jokes. There was a lot of laughing, a lot of drinking.

It was a warm evening and you were thirsty. You were determined to be careful and not drink too much, but you sort of lost track of the number of drinks you had. Then you lost track of the last half of the evening. You remember dancing and then sitting down and having this long profound conversation, coming up with all these deep and significant insights—except that you can't quite remember what they were.

However, there is one thing that you remember quite clearly. By the time you got home, you didn't feel very well—not very well at all. The worst part about it was the dizziness. When you lay down in bed, the whole room started spinning around—or was it just the bed that was spinning? Whatever was spinning, it was making you feel very nauseated.

You tried to get to sleep, but you felt too rotten. You had to keep getting up to go to the bathroom. Finally there were a few hours of oblivion. But now it's morning. You've opened your eyes. You try to sit up, and then you say to yourself, "I think I'm going to die!"

You have a hangover.

WHAT IS A HANGOVER?

There is no precise medical definition of a hangover. It's really a collection of symptoms that follow a bout of heavy drinking. Everyone experiences the hangover a little differently. But you don't have to define it to know what you have.

One of the most common symptoms of the hangover is a raging headache. The headache makes it painful for you to sit up or turn your head, and any quick motion is agony, as is a loud noise or a bright light.

The nausea and dizziness that started while the drinking was going on may still be present. You may also have diarrhea and a sore throat.

A surprising symptom is thirst. Though you have spent a night ingesting liquids, you feel completely dehydrated.

Extreme fatigue and emotional depression are also common in a hangover, and some people find that their muscles will tremble.

During a hangover you feel awful—you don't look too good either. The most familiar feature of the hangover is bloodshot eyes, and while your eyes may be red, your skin can be pale and blotchy.

Once experienced, a hangover is not something that

one forgets easily. It is a truly awful and degrading condition. At such moments remorse is common. You feel that you are being punished for your wickedness of the previous night, and you swear you will never, never do it again. However, a hangover is not moral retribution. It is a purely physical reaction to more of that toxic substance called alcohol than the body can handle.

Alcohol dilates—expands—the blood vessels, and too much alcohol overexpands the blood vessels, particularly in the brain. That's what causes the pounding headache.

The nausea and dizziness can be indications that there is plenty of alcohol left in your system; you are in fact still a bit drunk. The sore throat may be due to an irritation caused by the alcohol or by talking or singing loudly or by smoking too much or simply by spending a lot of time in a smoke-filled room.

As we noted, alcohol also stimulates urine flow, so that while you have drunk a great deal of liquid you have eliminated a lot too. The alcohol also redistributes the liquid in your body. More liquid moves to the outer layers of tissue—hence the thirst and feeling of dehydration.

The fatigue may be a general stress reaction to all the alcohol your body has had to deal with. You may also feel fatigued because you have not slept very much. Most drinking is done at night, and excessive drinking commonly takes place at late parties. We usually do not have the luxury of sleeping as late as we want the next day. Someone is going to come in and wake you up and ask you how you're feeling or yell at you for coming in so late and in such a condition. The light may wake you. You may simply have to get up to go somewhere. Besides, most of us operate with internal clocks. Our bodies are set to go to sleep at a certain hour and get up at a certain hour. We can't ignore these internal clocks completely.

Heavy drinking itself disrupts normal sleep. Sleeping is, of course, not simply a state of unconsciousness. During an ordinary night both our body and brain go through regular cycles. There is, for example, a regular cycle of dreaming. Sleep researchers have discovered that a person who is drunk does not dream the normal amount of time and, if extremely drunk, may not dream at all. There has been some speculation that delirium tremens, those terrifying hallucinations that sometimes afflict heavy drinkers, may be the result of extreme dream deprivation.

The bloodshot eyes come from dilated blood vessels in the eyes.

So now you know, at least in a general way, why you feel and look so awful "the morning after." But what you're really interested in is finding out what you can do about it. Is there any cure for a hangover?

THOSE HANGOVER CURES

Drinking lore is loaded with mythology, and there are probably more myths about hangover cures than anything else. Everybody seems to have his or her favorite cure and is more than ready to tell you about it or even help you try it when you are in the grip of a hangover. The eagerness of friends to help you cure your hangover can be almost ghoulish.

There is the "pick-me-up," usually some hideous-tasting concoction with bitters and hot sauce. If you can down the thing and keep from throwing up, it may take your mind off your headache for a moment, but that's only because the taste is worse than the headache.

A variety of vitamin preparations have been suggested, and excessive drinking over an extended period does bring on some vitamin deficiencies, but there is absolutely no evidence that massive doses of vitamins are going to help your hangover.

A raw egg, usually flavored with Worcestershire sauce or some other spice, is one of the legendary cures. It's a pretty ghastly concoction, even when you feel well; letting one of those slide down your throat while you are hung over can be memorably awful. It won't cure your hangover. Another slimy "cure" is a raw oyster with horseradish. It doesn't work either.

Breathing pure oxygen is supposed to be a cure, but an oxygen tank is not an ordinary household item. Besides, it will have no effect on your hangover.

Some robust soul will doubtless tell you that you'll feel much better after a hearty breakfast. Of course, if you were capable of eating a big breakfast, then you wouldn't be badly hung over in the first place. If you try to eat heavily, odds are that you won't be able to keep the food down, and you'll just feel worse.

In deference to the current emphasis on fitness, some suggest that a good jog is just the thing for your hangover. As with breakfast, if you can handle it at all, you're not that hung over, but it's not going to make you feel better.

Yet people swear by these and even more bizarre hangover "cures." The probable reason is what doctors call the "placebo effect," which means that if you really and truly believe something is going to make you feel better it may do just that—the effect, however, is entirely psychological. So if you do have faith in one of these cures, go right ahead.

There are, however, a couple of popular hangover cures that shouldn't be tried under any circumstances. One is the most legendary "cure" of them all, "the hair of the dog that bit you," that is, taking another drink. Since alcohol is a depressant, another drink may dull the pain a bit, but more alcohol is merely delaying the agony, not avoiding it. And those who keep on taking "the hair of the dog" can be headed for real trouble. If one delays the hangover by getting drunk all over again, and again and again, that is what is known as a binge. Eventually there is a crash that is far, far worse than an ordinary hangover.

Some people have tried to use tranquilizers or other pain-killing drugs, but this is extremely dangerous. Alcohol can have a deadly interaction with some drugs. The reactions are individualized and usually unpredictable. While you are hung over there is still plenty of alcohol in your system, so trying to cure your hangover with pills is playing a dangerous game. Don't try it.

The hard cruel fact is that there is no cure for a hangover. Eventually your body rids itself of the excessive alcohol and the various disruptions caused by the drinking calm down, but that takes time. Usually you will begin to feel better as the day goes on. A really severe hangover, however, can leave you feeling fatigued and queasy for several days.

EASING THE PAIN

While there is no hangover cure, there are a few things that you can do to ease the pain and discomfort. If you're a coffee drinker, then a cup or two might help because the caffeine constricts the blood vessels. Some people swear by black coffee; others say cream and sugar are necessary. Whatever way you're used to drinking coffee is probably best, because you already have an upset stomach, and there is no reason to give your stomach any more shocks.

The prescription drug ergotamine also constricts blood vessels, and some drug companies have manufactured hangover remedies containing both caffeine and ergotamine. Such medications may help the headache, but they won't do much for the other symptoms, and they will probably aggravate your nausea. It's a tradeoff most people would not wish to make.

Although you may want to stay in bed until the pain goes away, getting up may help your headache. That's because standing up will constrict those blood vessels. The old-fashioned ice bag on the head is also a help.

The dehydration can be extremely uncomfortable, and your first urge may be to gulp down a lot of water. If you do, you will probably throw up; too much water all at once will certainly increase your nausea and you'll feel dizzy as well. It's better to drink some hot, salty broth slowly. The hot broth is easy on the stomach, and the salt helps the body retain the needed fluid. It also provides some nourishment because you probably won't feel like eating for a while.

Tomato juice, a widely recommended "morning after" drink, may work for much the same reason, because most commercial tomato juice is salty. There is also some evidence that vegetable juices help to speed up the metabolizing of what alcohol remains in your system.

In addition to the mythology of hangover cures, there is also a lively folklore about ways to drink and not get a hangover.

There is, for example, the widely held belief that you can drink certain types of liquor which may make you drunk but won't give you a hangover. There is some evidence that congeners, various by-products of the fermentation or aging process that are found in alcoholic beverages, may increase the severity of the hangover. In general, the darker and more flavorful the liquor, the more congeners it has. Whiskey contains lots of congeners; that's what gives it a distinctive flavor. Gin and especially vodka contain very few. There are those who will tell you that you can drink all the vodka you like without getting a hangover the next morning. Don't try it. Perhaps a vodka hangover is less severe than one produced by whiskey—though this is by no means certain—but it can still make you feel terrible.

Some think that what really gets you is mixing your drinks, that is, first having a beer, then a whiskey sour, then rum punch, and so on. That combination might upset your stomach, but the real key is the amount of alcohol you take in, not the form in which it is taken. Generally, when a person has a lot of different kinds of drinks, it just means that he or she is drinking a lot.

Another commonly repeated bit of folklore is that it's not the liquor, but the mix, the orange juice, the ginger ale, or even the soda water that really makes you sick. Carbonated beverages like ginger ale and soda water actually speed up the intoxicating effects of alcohol. But in the end, you can't blame the ginger ale; it's still the alcohol. If you drink a lot of mix in an evening, that generally means that you have also taken in a great deal of alcohol as well. It is the mix that makes liquor palatable to most drinkers. If you tried to drink the liquor straight, you probably wouldn't.

The physical reactions to drinking are complex and highly individualized. You may well find that there are certain types of drinks to which you have a very bad reaction. Sometimes you can develop a psychological aversion to certain drinks. Just as there are some people who seem to get drunk very quickly, there are others who suffer severe hangovers after relatively modest drinking.

Obviously if you are one of those who react badly to alcohol, don't drink or drink very sparingly. Stay away from the stuff that makes you sick.

For everybody, the best way, indeed the only way, to avoid a hangover is simply don't drink too much or don't drink too quickly. A *very* general rule of thumb is that you probably won't get drunk or sick if you limit yourself to one beer, one glass of wine, or one cocktail an hour. And limit yourself to two or three in an evening. But we must stress that everyone reacts differently, and there are no ironclad "safe limits."

4

"Don't Tell My Folks"

*I*n a perfect world you wouldn't need this chapter. Parents and teenagers would talk things over sensibly and reach a friendly agreement on drinking. When parents said no, teens wouldn't drink. In turn, parents would practice what they preach, and their kids could never accuse them of being harsh hypocrites. But it is not a perfect world.

In the real world in which we live, the chances are, whether your parents condone your drinking or not, you've tried it, plan to try it, or at least feel strongly tempted. And, in the end, it's your choice whether or not you drink or how you drink, no matter what anybody else says. All the *no*'s, all the restrictions, all the lectures won't stop you.

You can't ignore your parents. You can't pretend that what they think has no effect on your life. Behavior, however, is not a one-way street; the way you behave affects the way they view you, and how you handle drinking can influence the way they treat you. So it's good for everybody if the lines of communication are kept open. And those lines run in both directions.

JOSHUA'S SIDE

Let's take a look at a typical case that may sound familiar to you, and let's see it from both sides of the generation gap. Joshua, sixteen, lives in a middle-class suburb. A junior in high school, he's in the upper 20 percent of his class academically, a member of both the ski team and the tennis team at school. He plays alto sax in band, is on the student council and the school newspaper. When it's time for college recommendations, Joshua's guidance counselor and teachers will send out page upon page filled with praise for the young man.

With all this to make his parents happy you can understand Joshua's anger at being told by his father to "put that damn thing back" the day he reached into the refrigerator for a beer. The temperature was up to ninety, and Joshua's father was sipping a gin and tonic at the time.

Nobody knows better than Joshua that his parents' lives are laced with alcohol. His father drinks regularly at lunch, "part of doing business." Not an evening goes by without a before-dinner cocktail. Wine is a regular feature of dinner. And when adults pay a visit, the first thing Joshua's parents ask is, "What will you have to drink?"

So when Joshua's father yelled at him for wanting one puny beer to quench his thirst, Joshua slammed out of the house. The man next door, who happens to be Joshua's math teacher, was heading for the mailbox, can of beer in hand. Actually, Joshua could not recall seeing his teacher out of school without a beer. As for his teacher's wife, she doesn't know what water is unless it comes with scotch. Yet Joshua was fully aware that were he to be caught in his very own front yard drinking by either his neighbor or his neighbor's wife, they would land on him like a ton of bricks and report him to his parents, as if he were a criminal.

Fuming at the injustice of it all, Joshua hurried off to see his grandfather, who lived around the corner. Joshua's grandfather was playing cards with some of his old cronies. They were drinking whiskey straight and swapping stories about the drunken escapades of their youth. Joshua's grandfather set the crowd roaring with laughter when he began bragging about how well Joshua's father could hold his liquor, but how when he was only sixteen he'd gone to a wedding and got so sloshed that he'd spilled booze all over the bride's white gown.

Upon hearing this, Joshua wondered why it was okay for his father to drink at weddings and special occasions when he was sixteen, but it was wrong for Joshua. Joshua was on the verge of throwing a fit.

Couldn't his parents see how hypocritical they were? Why shouldn't he, Joshua, have a good time now and then, drinking? Isn't drinking a rite of passage like getting a driver's license, a sign you're not a little kid anymore? Accumulating a store of drinking stories is part of the fun of growing up. There's a comic side to drinking, a fascinating mystique to alcohol. It isn't all morbid. Joshua had no desire to drink alone in his bedroom. He didn't get drunk in school. But he wasn't a baby. It was humiliating to see his parents blow up because he liked an occasional beer or went to a party where they spiked the punch. In a world swimming with alcohol he at least had a right to go wading in once in a while. Joshua decided the only thing to do was to go out that night and get drunk. If his parents didn't like it, too bad. If they couldn't respect his judgment, why should he respect theirs?

HIS PARENTS' SIDE

Okay, a lot of what Joshua says makes sense. But before you assume that his parents are completely wrong, here's the way they see it. It's illegal to drink at sixteen. This one hard fact simply will not go away. It's also illegal to serve alcohol to teenagers, and they are not the kind of people to go around idly breaking the law. If Joshua had permission to drink at home, he might decide to offer a friend a drink. If the friend was in an accident on the way home from Joshua's house, Joshua's parents would be blamed. They might be sued.

Even without the legal angle, there's the social pressure. If word got around that Joshua's parents considered it okay for their son to drink, other parents might start calling up and complaining. They might not let their kids come to Joshua's parties for fear there'd be liquor served. Over the past few years public attitudes have changed and hardened on the subject of teenage drinking. For all Joshua's talk about driver's licenses and rites of passage, had he been caught sneaking out driving the car when he was underage he would have been in one deep mess. He had to wait for his license until society decreed he was old enough to drive and the same holds for drinking.

Sure, Joshua's father drank when he was young. But behind all the bragging about exploits he nearly cracked up his car—and *that* he remembers even more vividly than the fun. Not to mention the times he made a fool out of himself, like the wedding he attended as a teenager where he spilled liquor all over the bride. That might sound funny now, but at the time it was an absolute nightmare. As for the hangovers, they weren't funny at all. So why shouldn't Joshua have the benefit of his father's experience?

Besides, Joshua's doing so well, why take a chance on his messing up? Adolescence is a time of radical mood shifts and wild risk taking. Kids don't always know when to stop. Alcoholism begins somewhere. It's just too iffy. Say yes to teenage drinking and you don't know what you might unleash.

Joshua's mother has another argument against Joshua's drinking. What would his sister, fourteen, and his brother, thirteen, think? Will they figure it's okay for them to drink, too? Better leave things the way they are now. No drinking allowed.

You may not like Joshua's parents' arguments against teenage drinking, but they aren't arbitrary. Both parents have thought a lot about the subject, and they are genuinely concerned. You can't just brush aside the fact that when you drink you're doing something illegal, and that your younger brothers and sisters are influenced by what you do. Do you really think it's okay for twelve-, thirteen-, and fourteen-year-old kids to sneak out in back of the middle school, the roller rink, or the bowling alley at night and get smashed? Early adolescence is tough enough. At that age one is growing and changing at a rapid rate and usually feeling very vulnerable.

One thing is sure: if Joshua comes home drunk, he won't change his parents' mind about drinking. His parents will probably decide that they were right to ban drinking in the first place, and Joshua will only feel more irritated than ever. No one will win.

Joshua might ask himself whether drinking is worth the fuss. You ought to ask yourself the same question. You don't really need to drink. It can wait. If your parents are generally reasonable people who respect your right to make decisions in many important areas of your life, why risk creating unnecessary strains just for an occasional binge or a beer now and then?

JILL

However, if you wince at the very idea of being the one person drinking soda at a party where everyone else is guzzling beer, at least play it smart. Don't do anything dangerous or foolishly antagonistic. When Jill, fifteen, came home from a party bombed, her parents began taking a lot closer look at where she went and whom she was with. After that, Jill was able to slip off to a party only when she lied to her parents and told them she was going to spend the night at the home of a girlfriend, somebody her parents knew and liked.

When Jill had friends over, they would raid her parents' liquor cabinet, then pour water into the bottles so her parents wouldn't guess. Then came the night her parents were out and Jill had a bunch of teens bring over a keg of beer. When Jill's parents came home early and walked into the middle of the party, it was explosion time.

There are a hundred ways parents can find out you've lied about where you were staying. Sooner or later parents will discover that their gin tastes as if it came out of the kitchen tap. Secret parties usually don't remain secret. At the very least neighbors and some of your friends' parents will know about them.

Even if you don't think you will agree with your parents, at least try to understand their concerns and feelings. You expect as much from them. Find out if your parents object to drinking chiefly on moral grounds. Or is it a matter of safety? Do they hate the idea of drinking *per se* or are they mainly concerned about your wrapping the car around a tree after a booze-soaked party? Of course, not all parents oppose all teenage drinking. Some find it acceptable under certain circumstances. Others actively encourage drinking, and that brings its own set of problems.

TOM

Tom, seventeen, drinks a lot. His father wouldn't have it any other way, though Tom's father is very strict when it comes to Tom's twin sister Nancy's having a drink.

Tom's father is a construction worker, and he likes to hang out with the guys in the bar after work. When he looks back on his own days in high school, he remembers all the good times he had at football games. Part of the fun was the drinking parties that followed. He wants Tom to have a good time too and to be strong and macho. That means, among other things, learning to hold liquor. Sodas are for kids; milkshakes are for weaklings. Real men drink booze.

Living up to macho standards can be very tough. Like most people, Tom has a sensitive side. He likes sports, but he also likes to draw. He enjoys the camaraderie of sharing a beer with the guys, but influenced by his father, he can't drink in an easy relaxed way. He always feels he has to prove something to himself. Like his father, he's trapped by the mystique of drinking.

Alcohol isn't just alcohol to Tom. It's the magic elixir that bonds friendships, makes heroes, shows who's tough, defines strength and self-worth. Though neither Tom nor his father are alcoholic, the amount of meaning they invest in taking a drink does pose a potential danger.

Anyone who drinks as heavily as Tom at seventeen

faces the risk of becoming dependent on alcohol psychologically or physically someday. Should anybody be concerned about Tom's macho attitude toward drinking? The answer is yes, because drinking has social ramifications. It's not just a private matter. When Tom climbs into a car drunk and turns on the ignition, he is everybody's problem. At parties he always encourages others to drink as much as he does. So, alas, the Toms of this world can't just be shrugged off.

MEG

It's easy to criticize Tom's father, but there are other kinds of problem parents, too. Some parents are so opposed to drinking they practically keep their kids under surveillance. Meg, fifteen, comes from a family with strong religious scruples against alcohol. Her parents never drink, and in their eagerness to prevent Meg from drinking, they hound her, smell her breath when she comes home from parties, invade her privacy by searching her room looking for hidden bottles. Meg feels as if she's a prisoner. She's torn between the teens at school who consider her a goody-two-shoes because she doesn't drink and her parents who hover over her waiting for her to try "the fatal glass of beer."

If Meg's parents continue to be rigid and unsympathetic, Meg may rebel and start drinking, even if she feels guilty about it. For her, as for Tom, liquor has a mystique, and again like Tom, Meg may have difficulty keeping drinking in perspective. Drinking, or not drinking, should not be central to anyone's life.

Don't write off Meg's parents as crazy fanatics. Understand that, even though they aren't dealing with the situation very well, their religious convictions are genuine and a source of strength to them. Meg's parents grew up in families badly disrupted by alcohol, which is one of the reasons they react fiercely to the very idea of drinking. Any kid raised in a family where one or both parents are alcoholics faces special problems, including severe emotional strains and sometimes even physical abuse. We are not saints; we're just human beings, and there is no way after what they've been through that Meg's parents can take a rational or calm view of drinking.

Does that mean Meg just has to suffer? Must she simply put up with excessive surveillance? When the issue of teenage drinking begins to tear a family apart, it's time to ask yourself whether that is just the tip of the iceberg. Drinking may also be the focus of deeper family problems. If you see yourself in this, then you ought to consider getting help through therapy or counseling.

Don't think your situation has to be as bad as Meg's to justify getting help. If the problem is that a member of your family is an alcoholic, there are organizations such as Al-Anon and Alateen geared to help you. To start, seek out an adult you trust, perhaps a guidance counselor, a minister, priest, or rabbi, or a teacher you like, and don't assume that all adults will simply give you a sanctimonious lecture about the evils of drinking. If your family can become involved, too, all the better; if not, do begin working things out for yourself.

For most teens the best way to cope with your parents about drinking is to behave responsibly. Don't drink and drive; don't make a habit of coming home bombed; and do stay in control. Your parents should be doing the same.

5

Party Time!

For most teens, drinking is a social—a very social—activity. A few drinks can put you at ease or make you behave like an idiot.

Finals were over, the night was warm. Prime time for a party! Like most of her friends, Maureen, seventeen, had spent hours getting ready for tonight. You never know what will happen at a party. You might meet somebody terrific. Was her hair okay? What about the color of her eye shadow? What should she wear? After changing clothes three times and staring once more into the mirror, Maureen was ready.

The party was at David's house, and his parties were famous. David's parents could care less how much drinking went on. Besides they never stayed home during parties. Of course, Maureen didn't tell her own mother this. She wasn't completely crazy.

Her friends arrived, and Maureen climbed into the car and took off. When they arrived at David's, they heard the sound of heavy metal booming on the soft spring air, matched only by the shouts of people jamming the house. Obviously, the whole world was invited to this party.

Maureen and her friends pushed past a crowd of strangers—David was somewhere, but nobody was quite sure exactly where—and headed for the punch. Then Maureen noticed a gorgeous guy across the room, and suddenly she felt so rattled and nervous that she grabbed a plastic cup of punch and started gulping. The punch was strong and tasted absolutely horrible, but it did the job. She began to feel much more confident. One more drink and she'd walk right up to that super-looking boy.

The doorbell rang, but nobody bothered to answer it, so a group of boys who had heard there was a party going on around here just walked in. They had a six-pack and a bottle of cheap vodka. As a joke they poured the vodka into the punch bowl and laughed.

Alex, fifteen, laughed louder than anybody else. To look at him, you'd think he was on his fifth drink, but he'd only had one. Just the atmosphere at the party, what with everybody drinking and joking, made him feel drunk. It was a good sensation, too, because for once in his life he was getting some attention. People had noticed him.

At school Alex was considered the biggest nerd in the class, or so it seemed to him. Short and skinny, he was convinced that nobody in high school had ever had more zits. But, thanks to the punch and the party, he was feeling taller and stronger and his complexion had cleared up. One more drink and maybe, just maybe, he'd get up the courage to talk to a girl, any girl.

In the bedroom, Jessica, sixteen, was sobbing her heart out. She'd gone from feeling good to being hopelessly depressed. Now she knew where the old saying "crying in your beer" came from. Gloomy thoughts kept popping into her head. She wasn't over Scott yet, even though they had broken up a whole month ago. She was flunking trig. This summer, instead of going away, she'd be working at a fast-food restaurant in the mall.

When David came into the bedroom and put his arms around her, she let all her misery spill out. David told her things weren't as bad as they seemed. She'd make it through trig. The mall was a great place to be in the summer, full of people. She could go to the beach on weekends.

Jessica was too bleak to be consoled, but she appreciated the sympathy, so when David kissed her she kissed him back. Actually she didn't like David very much, but she was too down to care whether they made out or not.

In the bathroom Christopher sat on the edge of the tub in totally gruesome shape. He felt nauseated and was on the verge of throwing up everything back to breakfast yesterday. It was hard to believe that out there near the punch bowl people were laughing. If you asked him, this party was sheer hell.

Ron was sprawled on the living room floor, drinking a beer and hoping he looked three years older. He was in eighth grade, while everybody else at the party was in high school. It was exciting to be at David's and flattering, too, but it was also a little intimidating. Here he was surrounded by sophomores, juniors, and seniors. Maybe another beer would help relax him. There was plenty in the refrigerator.

Paul, eighteen, downed drink after drink quickly. To him drinking was serious business. Now that he was a senior, he had moved beyond the traditional teenage party binge. He drank every night and during the day whenever anything got to him. It was taking increasing amounts of alcohol to make him feel good. Paul watched the others around him laughing and joking and considered joining in, but he decided he was okay alone. Plenty of time to socialize later. If he knew David, the party wouldn't break up till three in the morning.

Maureen had a 12:30 curfew, so she couldn't hang around till the party broke up. As she stepped over the people stretched out on the floor listening to music, she heard cars screeching up to the door. New people were arriving. Others were leaving, shouting and laughing, climbing into cars that roared off, sometimes to other parties.

The house was a terrible mess, positively disgusting. Crumpled cups had been tossed on the floor by a couple of slobs nobody seemed to know. Some idiot had tried to put his fist through the wall. Somebody else had thrown up on the living room rug. It was time for people to pitch in and help clean up before David's parents came home, but everybody was too drunk or tired to help. Besides, anybody in good shape was busy helping the ones who were drunk. Two of David's close friends had subdued a guy running around upstairs naked, dragging him into one of the bedrooms to put his pants on. Only they interrupted the couple making out in there. Somebody said it was two couples. This was turning into quite a party. Reluctantly, Maureen looked around for somebody sober enough to drive her home.

Janis, fifteen, hadn't had a drink all night, though she didn't want anyone to find out. So she walked around holding a glass of punch, occasionally pretending to sip it. Once or twice she went into the bathroom and poured the punch down the sink. Then she went back to the punch bowl, pointedly waving her empty glass so everybody would think she had just finished it off. At parties like this you were expected to love getting drunk. But Janis hated the taste of alcohol, and this punch full of cheap whiskey and whatever else was ghastly. Still, one of these nights she would have to break down and start drinking. Everybody else did. But at least tonight she'd gotten away with putting on a good act.

By 2:00 AM the party was over, and luckily it did not end in disaster. No one had an accident driving home, though Alex got a little overexcited and threw a rock through a store window. Christopher was sick the next day with a vicious hangover, and Ron was grounded when his parents learned where he'd been. A bewildered Jessica found herself going with David when she didn't want to, messing up her chances of getting back with Scott.

In school lore it was a dream party, one of the great ones. In reality, for a lot of people it was less than glorious. But that's how it goes with drunken parties. They're better in the telling than when you experience them. So if you're considering having one, think about what it will really mean.

For one thing there's the sheer damage to the house. You're not on your own yet, living in your own house or apartment. Do you think your parents will appreciate coming home to ring marks on the windowsill, a table broken because someone mistook it for a couch, and a rug permanently stained the color of punch?

Then there's noise. Neighbors become grouchy when they need three sets of ear plugs to sleep through a party. Expect complaints and figure the neighbors may never let you pick up a few bucks baby-sitting or mowing their lawn again.

If these seem minor problems, remember drinking parties tend to draw uninvited guests. In some cases these are kids too young for spiked punch, kids who may be drunk and sick for the first time in their lives at your house, leaving you to cope with a touchy situation. Some uninvited guests can be downright unpleasant. If the party is loud enough or your guests move from unpleasant to violent, you may just wind up with the cops at your door. Remember, practically everybody in the place is probably breaking the law by drinking. There will be unpleasant questions about where the liquor came from.

Worst of all, somebody is going to drive while drunk, risking the lives of everybody whether they've been drinking or not. Don't think you can sober up with a cup of coffee or with a walk in the fresh air. Only time rids your system of alcohol.

The best moments at parties often come when small groups sit around together talking quietly. That almost never happens with a crowd of people running around concentrating on getting smashed. Then there's peer pressure where teens egg each other on to get drunker and drunker. At this point, even the most exciting party can plunge downward and become depressing and dreary. As the night wears on, you'll see a lot of bad drunks, either hostile or weepy.

A PARTY, NOT A DISASTER

If you're planning a drinking party and your parents accept the idea, then at least try to make your party a safe, pleasant, and interesting one instead of a drunken bash. To begin with, don't hold an open party where just about anybody is welcome. Invite only your friends and people you'd like to know better.

Make sure your parents are home during the party. They don't have to hang around and get in the way, but they should make a brief appearance occasionally. Just their presence in the house will keep the party from spilling over into anything too crazy.

Make sure there's plenty of food at the party. Food slows the absorption of alcohol into the bloodstream. You can serve vegetables, dips, meat, cheese, pizza, crackers, even sweets. If they have the choice, some teens will pig out on chocolate rather than slosh out on liquor. You shouldn't encourage any guests to drink more than they want, so don't rush around filling up people's glasses. They'll get refills when they're ready.

Don't overdo the amount of alcohol in the punch and don't let anyone else add to it. Have soda, fruit juice, and club soda on hand so people have an alternative to drinking or can take a break from it. Remember, alcohol is absorbed much faster when you use a carbonated mixer like ginger ale, so if you're going to mix drinks, use fruit juice or just plain water instead.

If playing music and talking is enough for you and your friends, fine. But sometimes people drink too much or too fast at a party because social situations make them tense. Relax your friends by showing a movie on the VCR or watch videos. Have cards, Scrabble, trivia games, or Monopoly available so your guests won't just stand around getting drunk. Drinking should be secondary, never the primary purpose of a party.

If a party runs too long, even people who try not to will tend to drink too much. So end your party at a reasonable hour. And if at any time during the evening you notice someone guzzling too fast, try to stop them. They may feel great, but there's a delayed reaction to drinking, and they may already have had more than they should. People can go from happy to sick or sad before they know it when they drink quickly.

So far so good. You've behaved responsibly. But what do you do to prevent DWI (Driving While Intoxicated)? You can collect car keys at the start of your party and refuse to give them back later to anybody who's had too much to drink. You can see if your parents will agree to drive your friends home or ask guests to phone their own parents for rides. You can let people stay at your house overnight if they're not sober enough to drive.

One of the best ways of handling the problem is to have a couple of friends agree in advance not to drink at your party, so they can drive others home. If necessary, put someone in a taxi, even if you have to take up a collection to pay for it. Some of the teens at your party may have signed the SADD (Students Against Driving Drunk) contract. This reads: Teenager to parent: "I agree to call you for advice and transportation or both at any hour, from any place, if I am ever in a situation where I have been drinking, or if a friend or date who is driving me has been drinking."

But this is a mutual pact and it also says: Parent to teenager: "I agree to come and get you at any hour, any place, no questions asked and no argument at that time, or I will pay for a taxi to bring you home safely. I expect us to discuss this issue at a later time. I agree to seek safe, sober transportation home if I am ever in a situation where I have had too much to drink or a friend who is driving me has had too much to drink."

Since you will be a guest as well as a host and sometimes need a drive home yourself, you, too, should be thinking about the SADD contract and so should your parents. By the way, there is no need for your parents to embarrass you by coming to the door when they pick you up. Arrange to meet them in front of the house or even a few houses down. Some SADD chapters have students on call who will pick up teenagers after parties, no questions asked. Check and see if you have a similar program in your area. (For more about SADD, see chapter 13.)

Of course, there are always some parents who, whatever their intentions, pull their kids out of drinking parties in the most abrupt and insensitive way, making it difficult to call them. In some cases parents become so enraged over teenage drinking that teens prefer to risk driving home drunk rather than face a public confrontation. No one wants to be humiliated in front of friends.

If it sounds as if we're describing your parents, try to stay at a friend's after a drinking party or, if you can't work that out, let someone sober drive you home. Better to face a fight, particularly in private, than to be injured in a car crash.

PARTIES WITHOUT ALCOHOL

Are there any kinds of parties where liquor should not be available under any circumstances? Yes, any party that is an extension of an official school activity and where students as young as fourteen or under may be present, for example, drama club cast parties. Although the party may be at your house, it is not your party in the same sense as, say, a birthday party.

True, some school events do spawn a lot of drinking parties. Take senior prom and graduation. But parents and teachers no longer take a hands-off attitude to these celebrations and more and more schools are now holding all-night parties after proms and on graduation night. No drinking is allowed, but the school swimming pool is kept open, there's tons of food around, and rock bands play till dawn.

If your parents insist you too give parties without alcohol, don't despair. You can still have a good time.

Since Sandy's birthday came in October, she gave a costume party when she turned fifteen. Her parents argued strongly against her providing her guests with beer and wine, and though she put up a feeble resistance, she didn't really object. She was certainly no pro when it came to giving parties, and dealing with a drinking crowd would have been too much for her. Fortunately, everyone she invited got busy planning Dracula, ghoul, and ghost costumes, so they took the news there wouldn't be any drinking at the party calmly.

The costumes did for the guests a lot of what drinking does. Putting on a costume relaxes people, allows them to make a dazzling entrance, and puts everyone in a party mood. The shy hide behind masks, exhibitionists go all out, and even the people who are a little embarrassed about wearing a costume often enjoy it secretly.

Sandy and her closest friends decorated the house in a combination gruesome/comic decor. Sandy rented a couple of popular horror films like *Night of the Living Dead* and *The Attack of the Killer Tomatoes* for the party. A ouija board, a crystal ball, and fortune-telling cards were big hits, getting everyone joking around and sending weird messages.

Sandy also played an audio tape of *Rocky Horror Show*, the inspiration for many of the party's costumes. Then she served cake, not your usual red-rose-covered kind, but one decorated with black roses and a buttercream dagger.

After that, the mood switched from the horror theme to rock music, and everybody just chatted until midnight when the party broke up, with several girls staying overnight. All and all it was an unusual party and a lot of fun. No alcohol was necessary.

Of course if costumes aren't for you, there are other kinds of parties that work well without alcohol. You can go swimming, ice skating, or roller skating, or you can see a movie and then stop at the pizza place. Admittedly, as you reach your late teens, it gets harder to hold parties where nobody drinks. Your friends tend to be older. Some are probably out of high school, working, in college, or in the army. They may very well expect a beer or two. It's embarrassing if you can't provide them.

But you can still get away with giving parties where nobody drinks if your parents insist or if you prefer to keep it that way yourself. To carry it off graciously, keep the moralizing down. Don't come off as priggish, judgmental, smug, or morally superior because you're not having alcohol. Keep the party focus where it belongs—not on the absence of liquor but on having a good time. Then most people will simply accept having a soda instead of a beer and your party will be a success anyway. You have one thing going for you—heavy drinking is no longer considered chic or healthy. If your friends think you are being modern, not moralistic, they are much more likely to accept your restrictions.

6

Drinking Makes You Sexy! Or Does It?

There was a young lady from Kent,
Who said that she knew what it meant
When men asked her to dine,
Gave her cocktails and wine,
She knew what it meant—but she went.

Or as the American master of humorous verse Ogden Nash put it:

Candy is dandy,
But liquor is quicker

Perhaps you've seen those bumper stickers that read: Beer Drinkers Make Better Lovers.

That's one image of alcoholic beverages, a kind of aphrodisiac. Is it true? Does drinking make you sexy?

Everybody has heard stories about "drunken orgies," and a lot of teens have been to parties where somebody gets drunk, strips off his clothes, and starts groping the other guests. Rumors abound at just about every high school that "so and so" got drunk after the big game and slept with half the football team or posed for nude photographs after drinking too much.

Sometimes the stories are true, but often they're not or at the very least they are highly exaggerated. Much of what's considered outrageously drunken behavior is basically exhibitionism. Somebody shows off and makes an idiot out of himself or herself. You'd label these wild antics embarrassing, not sexy. As for the extreme stuff, such as the tales of drunken rapes, these are acts of violence. How much the alcohol is to blame and how much is due to other factors is difficult to say.

The idea that getting drunk makes you sexually powerful or energetic is false. As Shakespeare said of heavy drinking, it "provokes the desire, but takes away the performance."

Still, there's no question that a drink or two loosens inhibitions. Shy people start to talk. Someone who normally considers herself or himself unattractive may get a quick dose of "whiskey courage." And there are those who use alcohol as an excuse to do what they want to do anyway, blaming everything on a few beers. But they might find another excuse if liquor wasn't around.

If alcohol has the reputation of being "sexy" it's partly because that particular image has been promoted by manufacturers to sell their product. Take a look at what we mean. You turn on the television. You're looking at a posh Manhattan penthouse apartment, glitteringly modern and glamorous. A beautiful blonde, model-slim, in an expensive blue dress, sets out two crystal wine glasses. The crystal sparkles. The blonde's diamond earrings sparkle. Ice in a bucket on the table set for two sparkles.

The doorbell rings. The blonde answers it. The man who enters the room is elegant and handsome. What's more, he's wearing a tuxedo. Therefore, he must be rich. After all how many people do you know who go out on a date in a tuxedo? You can almost see the chauffeur-driven Rolls Royce that brought him to dinner. The blonde reaches for the bottle and a voice floats over the scene saying, "For that special superfantasy occasion make sure you serve ——— wine."

GETTING THE MESSAGE

You get the commercial's message. Wine is sexy. No romantic evening would be complete without it. What's more, rich people drink it. You don't want to be considered a poor dumb slob, do you? If you drink ——— wine, then maybe you, too, will somehow be more beautiful, more glamorous. Maybe the classiness displayed in the commercial will somehow rub off. If you're a guy, maybe you'll get a beautiful blonde. If you're a girl, maybe you'll grab a guy in a tux, one who rides around in a Rolls.

Not that you really believe all this. But the commercial succeeds in creating an aura, an image, a mystique. Advertising alone doesn't create the image. Many drinks come in attractive bottles, beautifully packaged. Barware is often appealing. Fancy restaurants serve liquor with style and flair. The rituals surrounding wine are very gracious.

Beer drinkers get hit with a different message, and when teenagers drink, beer is often their first choice. You switch on the television again. This time the screen is bright with a mellow sunset glow. A big strong macho construction worker in great shape is leaving his job. On his way to the neighborhood tavern he passes the harbor where a boatload of big strong macho fishermen in great shape have called it quits for the day. They, too, head for the neighborhood tavern. There they meet four major league pitchers and a basketball player. Everybody kids around and has a great time as a pretty barmaid appears carrying mugs of golden, frothy beer. Friendship, happiness, contentment radiate from the television screen. Real men, the commercial implies, drink beer. If you want to be big, strong, macho, sexy, and in good shape, then you, too, should drink beer.

SEXY OR FATTENING?

However, if you look closely, there's a real contradiction in the commercials. The glamorous blonde and the man in the tux are very, very thin. The guys in the beer ads are solid muscle. Not a beer belly in the lot. Most of them look as if they've been working out instead of sitting around the neighborhood tavern guzzling beer. And chances are, since most of them are models or actors, they have been exercising not drinking.

Over the past few years people have become more aware of the need to stay fit. Fat isn't chic. Neither is sagging softness. People jog, work out in gyms, play tennis, ride bicycles, roller-skate, take dancing lessons, attend exercise classes, swim, and ride horses just so they can be lean and muscular. Health is "in," and life-styles are changing drastically because of it.

High-tech types eat salads for lunch at fancy restaurants. Not long ago they would have devoured a three-course meal. The three-martini lunch is going out of fashion. Now it is one small glass of white wine or even a glass of mineral water with your lettuce. Despite the ads, the word is in that alcohol has plenty of calories. So if you're already guzzling the stuff as a teenager, figure by the time you're in your early to mid-twenties you'll be putting on weight. Of course, if you're an athlete and hope to remain one, that's an added reason for limiting the amount you drink.

MARK

Mark, eighteen, had always been good at sports. He'd joined the Little League and Pop Warner Football as a kid, often playing in championship games. In high school, he spent more time on athletics than on schoolwork because it was the most important thing in his life and what he was best at. Besides Mark wasn't dumb. He understood that though he'd never qualify for an academic scholarship, no matter how hard he studied, he'd probably be able to get an athletic scholarship.

Every Friday night Mark partied some and had a couple of beers. But most of the time he drank diet soda. He was proud of his strong muscular body and liked to wear T-shirts or walk around with his shirt off so everybody—especially girls—could admire his chest and shoulders. People said he was conceited, but he knew they envied him his looks and talents, so he didn't care what they said.

Besides, many of the people didn't realize how hard he had to work at staying in shape. While they were stuffing themselves on potato chips, he was eating salads. When they were out getting drunk on Saturday night, he forced himself to drink lightly. Sure he was tempted to get drunk, but the self-discipline was paying off. Colleges had started to recruit him.

Ten, maybe even five years ago, Mark would probably have been a heavy drinker. His friends would have expected it of him. Today a Nautilus machine, not a beer can, is Mark's symbol of prowess. A generation or so back Mark would probably have been a heavy smoker, too. Watch any old movie, and you'll notice that most heroes smoked. Today Mark is free to say no to cigarettes and most of the time to beer. So things change. Nowadays, moderation is sexy.

Girls as well as boys have been affected by the shift in values. Body building, which was once practically unheard of for women, has become not only acceptable but actually popular. Girls are as committed to exercise as boys and eager to stay thin. Just compare the ideal figure girls dream of having today to what was fashionable a hundred years ago. The famous beauty Lillian Russell is said to have weighed two hundred pounds! What would Tina, seventeen, and a mere 120 pounds, think of that?

TINA

The biggest worry to Tina is her weight. She's continually eating cottage cheese, doing aerobics, trying to lose ten pounds. Mostly she drinks fruit juice, skim milk, and diet soda. On Sundays she has a glass of wine with dinner. That's because Sunday is the time all the relatives get together at Tina's grandparents'. Her grandparents are from Europe, and though they've been in America for aeons, they still follow one of "the old country" customs and serve all the grandchildren above baby age a small glass of wine with dinner.

On an ordinary day Tina never even thinks about drinking. School, homework, and extracurricular activities keep her busy. She's editor of the school literary magazine. It's the second major interest of her life, next to losing weight. She writes short stories and poetry and presses other people to write short stories and poetry, since the magazine is supposed to come out more or less on time and there have to be four issues a year.

Every so often on a Friday night, Tina goes to a drinking party. She prefers movies, rock concerts, and of course, dates with fascinating boys, preferably blond, but she doesn't often strike it lucky. So she goes to parties. If the party is filled with grossly obnoxious people getting slobbering drunk, she generally gets bored and leaves. If the party is fun with good conversation, good music, romantic intrigue, and a chance to tell or hear some juicy gossip, Tina stays. She usually drinks a glass of wine early on to steady her nerves and put her in the right frame of mind for meeting boys. Tina believes a glass of wine brings out her sparkling side. With it, she's witty. Without it, she's a stuttering fool—or so it seems to her.

She usually drinks a second glass later in the evening, as she munches on celery and slices of green pepper. If the party is especially delightful, she may overdo it and drink too much, but she's only been bombed a couple of times, and for the most part she spaces her drinks carefully. Tina hates getting sick, and if she never has another hangover, that will be fine with her. She vividly remembers one particularly awful New Year's Eve when she guzzled her way to disaster. Mostly she sticks to club soda. With a splash of lime juice, it is elegant, bubbles like champagne, and best of all, has no calories. Tina is bound and determined to get down to 110 pounds yet, if it's the last thing she does.

So to sum up, a drink or two may help relax some people and add a certain ambiance to a romantic evening, though it certainly isn't essential. On the other hand drinking too much can kill a burgeoning romance fast. Throwing up on your shoes is not romantic. Neither is passing out. And while you might not remember making an ass of yourself, your date might. From the standpoint of acquiring habits that will last a lifetime, drinking is distinctly unsexy. Downing the stuff in large quantities can make you fat fast.

The main reason teens believe alcohol makes us sexy is that's the signal ads and commercials send. To look sexy, forget "a loaf of bread, a jug of wine, and thou." Be modern: make that "a glass of club soda, a thin, crisp rye cracker, and a free pass to the health spa." That may not be poetry, but it is a good guide to romance.

7

Beer, Wine, or Spirits

"*I*'m not drunk, I just had a coupla beers." We'll bet you've heard that one. Of course, it's not true, you can get very drunk on beer. But the opposite, which holds that all alcoholic beverages are the same, is not true either. Let's take a look at the most popular drinks in America today. At the top of the list is beer.

BEER

We Americans are not the biggest beer drinkers. The Germans and Australians drink more. But we do down over a billion and a half gallons every year. Next to water, beer is probably the most popular drink in the country. No matter what the ads say, we are not the Pepsi generation.

Beer varies a good deal in taste, appearance, and alcoholic content. The most popular beers in the United States today are lagers, a form of light, clear beer that was first popularized in America by German immigrants in the mid-nineteenth century. Virtually all of the well-known brands of American beer are lagers. Some are called pilsner, after a very popular beer that was brewed in the town of Pilsen in Czechoslovakia. Pilsners are generally somewhat lighter in flavor and clearer in color than the standard lager.

Today what once would have been called a pilsner is commonly called a "light" beer. Light beers have been heavily advertised and are extremely popular primarily because people believe that you can drink them without getting fat or drunk. They are lower in calories than the standard lagers, under 100 calories per twelve-ounce can as compared with about 125 for a lager. But they are certainly not diet drinks. Some people like the taste; others find it flat and uninteresting. The alcoholic content of light and regular beer, however, is just about the same. If drinking light beer encourages you to drink more, you will take in more calories and get drunker than on standard beer.

Before the mid-nineteenth century what we now call ale rather than beer was the most common drink in America—though at the time it too was often called beer. Ale tends to be fuller bodied and richer in consistency than today's beer. In reality, most commercial ales today differ only slightly from beer.

Bock beer is a dark rather sweet beer that traditionally was available only in the spring but is now available year round. As with most other modern beers, it is no longer as distinctive as it once was.

There are a number of other dark beers available, and some are merely darker in color. But the dark beer called stout, which is popular in England but widely available in the United States, is very dark and has a distinctly strong and sweetish taste. It is also considerably more alcoholic than most beers. Porter, which is not widely available in the United States, is a dark form of ale, sweet and very foamy. Stout, porter, and many English ales are commonly drunk at room temperature rather than being chilled.

A variety of beverages called "malt liquors" are really beer with a strong flavor and higher alcoholic content. They are sold under several different brand names and have a steady popularity in the United States.

Beer varies a good deal in alcoholic content, but most American beers contain between 4 percent and 5 percent alcohol. Compare that with about 12 percent for table wine and 40 percent to 50 percent for spirits. Malt liquors and many imported beers contain considerably more alcohol, as much as 8 percent. So if you're drinking an unfamiliar brand of beer, you might be surprised by the "kick" that it contains.

At one time Americans drank a very weak beer—often home brewed. It was popularly called "small beer," and it was never really popular. Indeed the phrase "small beer" came to mean something of no importance. A low-alcohol beer that people called "near beer" or 3.2 beer because its alcoholic content was 3.2 percent, just below the legal limit for a controlled beverage, was sometimes sold on college campuses and other places where young people gathered. It could, of course, be sold legally to drinkers of any age, and it was very difficult to get drunk on 3.2 beer. But "near beer" was always regarded as a very poor substitute for the real thing.

Recently several varieties of nonalcoholic beer have been imported from Europe and are being widely promoted in the United States as the kind of beer you should drink when you shouldn't be drinking. Whether the product will catch on remains to be seen. In the meantime, we have heard it referred to as "kiddie beer" and children ten and under have been drinking it, presumably to imitate their elders. If the chief market for these nonalcoholic beers turns out to be little kids, then the product will surely face heavy criticism as a substance that gets children into the habit of beer drinking.

Brewing

Brewing is a fairly complex process, and slight variations in ingredients or timing can produce major variations in the final product—anything from light beer to stout. Brewing is carefully controlled so that each type of beer retains its own distinct characteristics.

Beer begins with barley and other grains. The grains are sprouted, dried, and transformed into what is known as malt. The malt is ground up and mixed with water, producing the product known as mash. The mash is cooked, and the liquid, called wort, is filtered out. Flowers or cones from the hop vine (hops) are added to give the beer flavor. The mixture is boiled for a few hours, and at this point yeast is added to begin the fermentation process, the chemical action that changes the starch in the mixture to alcohol.

Brewing a batch of beer used to take months, but in modern breweries the time has been reduced to three or four weeks. Brewing has probably changed more than the making of wine or spirits. In most modern breweries the entire process is controlled by computer, but not too many years ago the operations of a brewery were under the supervision of a highly skilled and experienced brewmaster who used his experience and instinct to make sure that each step was done correctly. Some beer enthusiasts believe that the mechanization of brewing has reduced both the quality and the interest of beer. At one time there were hundreds and hundreds of local brands of beer, each one different from the other. Today the beer industry is controlled by a few large national breweries that market their products throughout the nation. Most of the local brands are long gone, and one can get the same glass of beer in New York, Houston, Chicago, or Los Angeles. There has, however, been a jump in the number of imported beers sold in the United States.

Most beer today comes in cans or bottles. Kegs of beer are used in taverns where beer is sold by the glass. This "draft" or "tap" beer is slightly different from the bottle or can variety of the same brand.

Barley is not the only grain used in the brewing of beer; indeed, beer or beerlike drinks can be made from a number of different grain products. The Japanese drink saki, which is commonly called rice wine, is really closer to being rice beer. Saki is served heated, in tiny cups, but don't try to drink too many of them, for saki's alcoholic content is much higher than that of ordinary beer.

Of the three major classes of alcoholic beverages—beer, wine, and spirits—beer has, by far, the lowest alcoholic content. There also appears to be something about beer that inhibits the effect of the alcohol, so that if you ingest an equal amount of alcohol from beer or vodka, the vodka will probably make you a little drunker, a little quicker. But don't count on it. There are plenty of people who just can't drink very much beer because they feel bloated almost immediately. But for most, beer is a refreshing drink, one that goes down easily and pleasurably, so that one tends to drink a good deal of it.

Public attitudes toward beer have varied dramatically. During the last century in England and America, beer was often looked upon as a healthful beverage, far better for the working man than gin or rum. Indeed, there was some question as to whether beer was an intoxicating beverage at all. In America there was resentment against beer because those who brewed it were generally "foreign." Today vodka-guzzling Russians consider beer an antidote to drunkenness (it isn't). On the other hand, beer has been denounced as the most insidious and dangerous of all alcoholic beverages. But even in the antidrinking movement this is a minority view, except in regards to teens. Among teens beer is widely drunk and thus widely denounced.

WINE

Wine is an ancient and fabled drink. Volumes have been written about it. Poems have been inspired by and dedicated to it. There can be a ritual surrounding the drinking of wine that is more elaborate than the Japanese tea ceremony. It is a drink of truly mythic proportions. It's not just something cheap you guzzle down to get high.

Basically wine is fermented grape juice. There are drinks called wine made from berries, cherries, pears, even dandelions, but these are heavily sweetened oddities. The true source of wine is the grape.

After that simple statement the subject can become very complex. There are a huge variety of wines, and they can be classified in scores of different ways. Let's start by breaking wines into two main groups, table wines and fortified wines.

By far the most common are the table wines. These are naturally fermented grape juice, whereas the fortified wines have something added. Table wines are generally meant to be drunk with meals, hence the name.

To make wine, the grapes are picked and crushed. At one time the grapes were tossed into a large vat and crushed by barefooted peasants who stomped on them. While there are still a lot of jokes about crushing grapes with your feet, and that practice may be preserved in a few remote places, most modern wine making is highly mechanized and scientifically controlled.

After the grapes are crushed, the skins, seeds, bits of vine, and other solid material float to the top. The juice, or must, that remains is what eventually becomes wine. The must is drawn off, placed in casks, and stored in a cellar or warehouse for months or years, depending on the type of wine. After the wine is bottled, the fermentation process may continue, so wine connoisseurs will store bottles of wine for months or years after they have been purchased, in order to improve their flavor, body, aroma, and color. Wine can, however, remain in the bottle too long and lose its desirable qualities; it is then said to be "dead." Wine lovers regard their favorite beverage as very nearly a living thing.

Table Wines

There are a number of ways of classifying table wines, including dry and sweet. Dry really means nonsweet; the majority of table wines are dry. Then there are red and white wines, as well as pinkish wine called rosé, and a new classification of very slightly pink wines called blush. The color of a wine depends primarily on the type of grape used to make the wine. Red grapes make red wine; white grapes make white wine. Actually, neither the grapes nor the wine are truly white, but they are relatively colorless.

Within these broad classifications there are almost infinite variations. There are many varieties of both red and white grapes. The final wine can be affected by the amount of time it is aged, the place where the grapes are grown, the weather during the year in which the grapes were grown, the type of cask in which the wine is fermented, the skill and taste of the wine maker, and so forth.

Traditionally wines, particularly French wines, are grown, aged, and bottled on the same estate. Only a particular type of grape grown in a particular year in a particular place is used to make a bottle of fine wine, and the information is found on the label, for example "Chateau Margaux, 1968." Wines of this type from a celebrated vineyard and from a good year—that is, a year in which growing conditions were considered exceptionally favorable—can be astronomically expensive.

There are those who are skilled and experienced enough to be able to identify wine from a particular vineyard and even from a particular year by the taste, bouquet (roughly, the way it smells), and color alone. Becoming a wine expert takes time and money, but many regard it as the mark of a truly cultured individual.

Most of us, however, can't tell the difference between a five-dollar bottle of California red and a bottle of vintage bordeaux from France costing ten times as much. Indeed there are those who claim there is no difference, certainly no difference great enough to justify the vast difference in price. People who sniff corks and make comments about a wine being "modest yet bold," say the critics, are nothing more than wine snobs. We won't get into that argument, for it is certainly a matter of taste, and taste alone.

It's not an argument we need worry about either, for fine estate-bottled wines are beyond the budget of the vast majority of us, except on the most special of special occasions. And then a fine wine should be drunk with a fine meal. If you don't know much about wine, but figure you really want to do something special and spend a bundle on a fancy French wine to go with your pot roast, you're almost certainly going to be disappointed.

Modern Wines

The table wines that most of us encounter are blends. That is, they are made from the grapes grown in different years from many different vineyards. The wine is not fermented in the cellars of the chateau but in large modern plants, where chemists keep track of fermentation and are able to insure a uniform quality. Mass production of wine has robbed the drink of much of its individuality, but it has also saved the public from the really terrible wines that were once regularly dumped on the market. You couldn't tell you had an awful wine until you opened the bottle, and then it was too late.

The names of the wines are more confusing than ever. A wine called bordeaux may be produced in Algeria or California, not in the Bordeaux district of France. A chianti from New York State may not taste at all like a chianti from the small district in central Italy where the wine originated. Many wine drinkers will find a couple of basic wines that they like and then will occasionally experiment with others.

From Thomas Jefferson on, there have been those who have urged Americans to drink wine rather than other alcoholic beverages, because wines are supposed to be drunk slowly with meals and thus are less intoxicating. Besides, wine drinking is considered a sign of civilization. In recent years wine drinking and the production of American wines have been on the rise. But unlike most European countries where red wines are most popular,

Americans have preferred white wines, often as a substitute for cocktails.

This has been hailed as a sign that people are starting to drink more moderately, and that might be the case. But there are potential problems. White wines have just about the same alcoholic content as reds, between 7 percent and 14 percent. The reds generally have more flavor and are almost invariably drunk with meals. White wines are usually drunk chilled, often before meals. Some are so "light" that they almost taste like water and can be downed just about as quickly. Though white wine may look and taste mild enough, when drunk in quantity without food it can make you very drunk indeed.

There are also the sparkling wines, of which the best known is champagne. Real champagne and other top-quality sparkling wines are produced a little differently from table wines. A small amount of sugar is added, and they undergo a second fermentation in the bottle. The gas produced by this fermentation is sealed in the bottle and released in the form of bubbles when the bottle is opened. Cheaper sparkling wines are made by forcing carbon dioxide into them.

Sparkling wines are very festive. The cork (or plastic stopper) pops. The wine may bubble out, and as we have mentioned, the effect of the alcohol hits you more quickly than with practically any other drink. Champagne is the traditional wine for celebrations and is supposed to be the drink of the very rich. Real champagne, that is made in the Champagne district of France, is very expensive, although it is by no means the most expensive wine available. There are a large variety of sparkling wines that are called champagne produced in New York, California, and elsewhere. There are also other sparkling wines, such as asti spumante, sparkling moselle, sparkling burgundy, and cold duck, just to name a few.

Wine connoisseurs (or wine snobs) usually contend that the really expensive champagnes are just a waste of money. Unlike fine red wines, which improve with age, champagne will go flat or become vinegary in a few years. Besides, they say, champagne is really a fairly simple wine, not the sort of drink that is savored or lingered over.

For years people have been mixing wine with soda water to make wine coolers or spritzers. The drinks have proved so popular that they have begun to appear premixed in bottles and cans. Wine coolers are now sold in six-packs, an attempt to rival beer. Ordinary wine can also be sold in aluminum cans, but this form of packaging has never caught on in America, though with the growing popularity of the wine cooler that may change.

Another wine mix is sangria, wine combined with fruit and fruit juice. This too has proved so popular that it comes premixed. Wine coolers, because they contain a large percentage of nonalcoholic soda water, tend to be fairly low in alcohol, about 5 percent, or the same as beer, whereas sangria, which has a larger percentage of wine, is correspondingly higher in alcohol. Both of these drinks, like white wine, tend to be so easy and pleasant going down that people forget that they contain any alcohol at all—but they do.

Vermouth is a wine that is flavored with herbs. The wine base differs depending on whether the beverage is supposed to be sweet or dry. In Europe, vermouth is often drunk straight, whereas in the United States it is most commonly used as a mixer or in cooking.

There are a large number of "novelty wines" or "pop wines" with names like Ripple and Thunderbird, which are sweetened or flavored in some way. These are often quite cheap because the sugar and the flavoring are used to cover the harsh taste of the poor quality wine itself. Because they are so cheap, and because they can taste more like soda than they do like wine, such wines are often attractive to new drinkers. They are also often pretty high in alcoholic content. Though we can cite no studies, simply talking to people who have overindulged with these cheap wines has given us the impression that they can make you just about as sick as any drink you can imagine. Be careful with them.

Fortified Wines

Some of these novelty wines might properly fit into the last great classification of wines, the fortified wines. Fortified means that the wine has been strengthened by the addition of more alcohol. Fortified wines contain 18 percent to 20 percent or more alcohol. Wines weren't fortified just to make them more intoxicating. The alcohol also helps to preserve the wine. At one time when transportation was slow and bottling uncertain, most wines had to be drunk near where they were produced. Attempts to ship wine would often cause it to spoil somehow. Even today it is said that some wines don't "travel well." Add alcohol, however, and the casks of wine could be stored in the hold of a ship, take a long sea voyage, and arrive tasting just as they had when they had been poured into the cask.

Shakespeare's drunken knight Sir John Falstaff drank sack—a fortified wine from Spain that we today call sherry. The most popular wine in colonial America was madeira, a powerful fortified wine from the island of Madeira. British gentlemen of the Victorian era would always have a glass or two of port—a fortified wine from Portugal—after dinner.

Though improved methods of transportation and storage have reduced the need for fortified wines, they are still around because people like the taste, though they are certainly nowhere near as popular as they once were. Dry sherry, sometimes poured over ice, is often drunk in place of a cocktail either before dinner or anytime cocktails are taken. All the sweet dessert wines that bear names like sherry, madeira, and port, though they may no longer come from Spain, Madeira, or Portugal, are fortified wines.

DISTILLED SPIRITS

Whereas beer is the most widely drunk alcoholic beverage and wine the most honored, distilled spirits are the most varied. We can only discuss the principal types here, but first, a few general points. Distilled spirits, or hard liquor as they are commonly called, are all produced from fermented grain, vegetable, or fruit juice—the starting point may be grain, sugar, grapes, or potatoes. Distillation changes the chemical content of the liquid, but what is most important from a practical point of view is that it raises the alcoholic content. If distillation goes on long enough, the result will be pure or nearly pure alcohol, a colorless, odorless, and almost tasteless "neutral spirit." Pure alcohol would burn like the devil if you tried to drink it.

While the alcohol in beer and wine is measured in percentages, spirits are measured in proof. Thus 100 proof means 50 percent alcohol by volume. Most spirits run between 70 and 100 proof, although there is a rum that is 150 proof.

Whiskey

The popularity of whiskey in America has declined from the days when a tax on it was enough to set off a revolt and whiskey was downed straight, by the cupful. It has even declined in popularity over the last ten years, from the days when good scotch whisky was considered the prestige drink. But whiskey still remains the best-selling type of hard liquor in America.

There are many different varieties of whiskey—all made from grain. Any grain can be used, but in America the important grains are corn (maize) and rye with some millet, sorghum, and barley. The grain is first "mashed"—diluted with water and cooked. It is then left to ferment into what is called "distillers' beer." After fermentation, the "beer" is pumped into stills for distillation and rectification; the "beer" is heated, so that water and impurities are separated from the alcohol. The product of the distillation is between 70 percent and 90 percent alcohol. After the distillation, it is diluted and aged, then diluted again to between 80 proof and 100 proof and bottled.

The most famous American whiskey is Bourbon, originally made only in Bourbon County, Kentucky. By law Bourbon must be distilled from a mash of at least 51 percent corn and aged for not less than four years in charred oak barrels. Rye whiskey starts with a mash of at least 51 percent rye and does not have to be aged in charred barrels.

The legendary illegal whiskey of the South is corn whiskey, sometimes called corn likker, white lightnin', or moonshine. It is distilled from a mash containing at least 80 percent corn and is aged little if at all. It's colorless and so harsh and raw that people who have not grown up with it generally find it undrinkable. A less potent corn whiskey is available legally, but there is not a big market for it.

Whiskey can either be straight or blended. Straight whiskey is what comes out of the barrel at the end of the aging process. Blended whiskey is 20 percent straight whiskey mixed either with other whiskey and/or grain alcohol. Blended whiskey is cheaper and lighter, but it can also be pretty foul tasting.

Canadian whisky is whiskey distilled in Canada under rigid government supervision. It's popular worldwide. A century ago the most popular whiskey in the world was probably irish whiskey, which, as the name implies, is whiskey made in Ireland. Peter the Great of Russia was reputed to have said, "Of all wine, only Irish wine is the best"—there is, of course, no Irish wine, only irish whiskey, and that's what the Czar liked. In Ireland where taxes on liquor are high, moonshining is a widespread occupation, and the illegally distilled spirit is called "poteen," after the small and easily dismantled pot still in which it is made.

Until about a century ago scotch whisky was almost exclusively for the Scots. It was sometimes called malt whisky and was made entirely from malted barley distilled slowly in pot stills. It was high in proof, very distinctive in flavor, and outside of Scotland itself, expensive and difficult to obtain. But then the Scots learned how to blend their whisky and yet retain the distinctive scotch flavor. Most scotch whisky in America is of the blended variety, although a few very expensive single malts have made their way to the American marketplace. Blended scotch should not be confused with cheap blended whiskey.

For much of the twentieth century, scotch whisky was

considered the king of spirits, but recently it has been losing its popularity, with disastrous results to parts of the economy of Scotland.

Gin

As we mentioned, any spirit can be distilled to the point where it loses its original characteristics and becomes a colorless, tasteless (though highly alcoholic), "neutral spirit." Gin starts with such a neutral spirit, usually made from grain, though sometimes gin has been distilled from molasses. The spirit is then redistilled with juniper berries or other flavorings. It requires little or no aging. Gin is comparatively easy to make, and that's why one of the most popular liquors of the Prohibition era was called "bathtub gin." It is also relatively inexpensive to produce and can have a high alcoholic content. Thus it has frequently been the drink of the poor and the desperate. In England in the eighteenth century, gin had a bad reputation because it was cheap and highly intoxicating. In America at that time, "demon rum" had the same reputation for the same reasons. There are, in fact, several different varieties of gin, of which Dutch gin is probably the most distinctive. But in general Americans do not drink gin straight (though the Dutch do). Neutral almost tasteless gins are preferred as bases for mixed drinks like martinis or collinses or drinks made with tonic water.

Vodka

No matter what turn international politics may take, nothing seems to have slowed America's growing infatuation with that most Russian of drinks, vodka. Vodka is the most neutral of all the spirits. It is often nearly tasteless and odorless. Unlike gin, it is unflavored and thus a popular base in drinks for people who do not really like the taste or smell of liquor. In the Soviet Union vodka is drunk straight, tossed right down the throat before dinner, after dinner, or practically any other time. This is done so regularly that alcoholism has become a problem of major concern to the Soviet government, and they have tried stern measures to stem the flow of vodka to their own people.

Vodka is now manufactured all over the world. Traditionally it was made from potatoes, but most vodka is made from grain spirits today, particularly in the West.

Rum

Rum is distilled from the fermented products of sugarcane. Of all the spirits, rum keeps the most of the natural taste that comes to it from its product of origin. In spirits such as whiskey and vodka the potatoes or grain have to be malted, that is, cooked and mashed first, in order to convert the starch to sugar. With sugar-based rum no such process is necessary. The distillation of rum is relatively easy, and some varieties of rum do not even have to be aged for very long. Thus rum is one of the simplest spirits to produce and in places like the West Indies, where sugarcane is abundant, one of the cheapest to produce. Indeed, rum originated in the West Indies, and for many years it was the standard drink of the American colonies and the British navy.

Though most school history texts ignore this, the American colonists were far more upset over the tax on rum than they were over the tax on tea, because they drank a lot more rum than tea. There is a story that Paul Revere started his famous ride in morose silence until he reached the home of Isaac Hall, captain of the minutemen and a rum distiller. After a couple of glasses, Revere began to shout that the British were coming. The story may be exaggerated or completely untrue, but rum certainly was the drink of choice among Americans of that era.

There is a wide variety of rums available, usually labeled by the island of their origin, Puerto Rico, Jamaica, or Barbados. But most people judge rum by whether it is light or dark. In general, the darker the color of the drink, the heavier, more flavorful the taste. Rum can range in color from mahogany to very nearly colorless.

Originally rum was drunk straight, and the fuller-bodied darker varieties were preferred. Over the last forty years or so there has been a strong trend toward the lighter rums. Most Americans never touch straight rum of any kind, but prefer it in a variety of mixed drinks, usually highly sweetened ones.

Brandy

Technically the word *brandy* means distilled wine, and indeed that is what most brandies are. However, the word has also been appropriated to apply to distilled spirits made from apples, pears, cherries, blackberries, and so forth. The brandies distilled in the Cognac region of France are considered to be the best in the world. American apple brandy is known as applejack, and a French brandy made from apples or pears is called calvados. Some fruit brandies are extremely sweet, more like syrups than drinks.

Cordials and Liqueurs

The words *cordial* and *liqueur* are virtually synonymous, and they refer to the sweet, usually strongly alcoholic drinks that traditionally are served in very small glasses after dinner and are made of sugar syrup and spirits flavored with plants, fruit, or herbs. There is an enormous range of flavorings used in liqueurs. Cointreau, for example, is made with orange peel soaked in brandy and other unnamed components. Benedictine is made with a secret formula that has been jealously guarded by the monks of Normandy for centuries. Aniseed is the principal flavoring of the anise liqueurs, caraway in kümmel, peppermint in crème de menthe.

Some liqueurs are favorites among young drinkers because they are so sweet and candylike, but be warned. Though they may taste like a milk shake, they contain a great deal of alcohol, and because of all the other ingredients, when drunk in quantity they are capable of making one extremely ill.

This discussion hardly exhausts the subject of spirits. There is for example the Mexican drink tequila, distilled from the juice of a cactus, and slivovitz, a colorless plum brandy that is a favorite before- and after-dinner drink in central Europe. Aquavit is a Scandinavian spirit flavored with caraway seed. In Greece there is ouzo, a colorless anise-flavored drink often taken as an aperitif, or before-dinner drink, though Greeks will drink it anytime. In France a similar drink is called pernod. Absinthe is an extremely potent light green spirit that is now banned in most countries in the world because one of the ingredients is the poisonous herb wormwood. The drink, however, is still widely available in Spain, where in the words of wine expert Alexis Lichine, "the dangers of absinthe will be hotly denounced over full glasses of the cloudy liquid."

8

A Brief History of Booze

Alcohol, the stuff that gives drinks their kick, is the result of a process known as fermentation. Fermentation, which converts starch and sugar into ethyl alcohol, occurs naturally and often in all sorts of materials. The first alcoholic beverage was probably downed quite by accident by a prehistoric man or woman who drank a substance that had been left around too long and had begun to ferment. He or she may have liked the taste and/or the effect that the drink produced. Eventually people were not content to rely on accidental fermentation but were deliberately producing alcoholic beverages. By the time we enter the era of recorded history our ancestors were fermenting an impressive variety of substances.

The earliest alcoholic beverage to be widely used may have been mead, made from fermented honey. Grapes for wine may have been among the earliest crops ever cultivated, and it has been suggested that people first changed from a nomadic to a settled way of life because they had to stay in one place until their grapes ripened. Scenes of the brewing of beer have been found on pottery from Mesopotamia that is at least six thousand years old. In ancient Egypt the honor of brewing beer was given to the high priests, who offered their product not only to the populace at large but also to the gods themselves.

Genghis Khan and his hordes drank fermented mare's milk called koumiss, whereas in India a drink called arrack was made from palm juice. The Aztecs concocted their brew from cactus sap, and in addition to making beer from grain, the Egyptians made wine from dates. Coconuts, potatoes, peaches, dandelions, pumpkins, and persimmons have been made into drinks. If a substance can be converted to a liquid and fermented, someone, somewhere, has undoubtedly tried to drink it.

So people have consumed an enormous variety of alcoholic beverages for many different reasons. The obvious one is to quench thirst. The intoxicating effects of alcohol have always been used to promote good cheer and fellowship or in the face of disaster at least to produce oblivion. "Give strong drink unto him that is ready to perish, and wine unto those that be of heavy heart. Let him drink, and forget his poverty, and remember his misery no more" (Proverbs 31:7).

Alcoholic beverages have been used to preserve foods and to improve their taste. They have been used as medicines for practically everything that ails you and, in the days before anesthesia, to dull the pain of an amputation. Wine has often been a sacramental agent in religious ceremonies. Sometimes intoxication has been regarded as a way of reaching the divine.

The Greeks, who preached moderation in all things, loved their wine and formed drinking clubs that often grew into powerful political factions. The Greek god Dionysus, whom the Romans called Bacchus, was the patron of wine. Dionysus was also the center of a secretive but very widespread and exclusively female cult that involved wild, abandoned revels. Since little is authentically known of the rites of Dionysus, we cannot be sure if the celebrants worked themselves into a frenzy with the aid of alcohol, but the image of the drunken bacchanalian orgy is one that is stuck in our minds.

The Bible, both Old Testament and New, has a lot to say about drinking—much of it good. The drinking of wine was, in general, an accepted part of life of the people of biblical times. Wine was served at the Last Supper. While drinking was accepted, drunkenness was not. Noah, who by tradition planted the first vineyard, overindulged and "was made drunk and was uncovered in his tent"— a great shame. And Proverbs warns, "The drunkard and the glutton shall come to poverty." Proverbs also warns that kings should not take strong drink lest they forget their duties.

Some religions forbid drinking entirely. The Koran is very clear about this, and in some nations where Muslim fundamentalism has a stronghold, it can literally be worth a person's life to try to get a drink. In Buddhism and some branches of the Hindu religion, drinking is strongly discouraged.

DRINKING IN AMERICA

In the West, however, total abstinence has rarely been considered a possible or even a desirable state. Someone who frowns upon drinking is today often called a puritan, yet the real Puritans were not abstainers. Drunkenness was quite common among God's Saints, and while public drunkenness might be condemned and punished, drinking itself was not. In the late seventeenth century the

Reverend Increase Mather, probably the most influential Puritan minister of his time, said that drink was "a good creature of God" and that man should partake of the gift without abusing it. He warned, however, that a man must not "drink a Cup of Wine more than is good for him."

His equally influential son, the Reverend Cotton Mather, was somewhat more concerned by the prospect of drunkenness. While Cotton Mather never condemned the practice of drinking in general, he did worry that excessive drinking might pose a threat to the established social order. He encouraged people of the "Best Sort" to set a good example by not getting drunk.

The warnings of Mather and others like him may have had some effect on the amount of drinking in New England, though even this is by no means cetain. However, throughout much of the rest of the American colonies, men, women, and even children were downing stupendous quantities of highly potent hard cider and rum, without restriction and without guilt. In 1744 Dr. Alexander Hamilton of Annapolis traveled throughout the colonies recording his observations. He deplored the fact that the people of Philadelphia didn't seem to drink enough, but in New York he found that heavy drinking was essential in good company. Governor George Clinton, "a jolly toaper" in Dr. Hamilton's view, matched him drink for drink. But the endless New York toasts were too much even for Dr. Hamilton, who said he preferred to limit himself to a single bottle of wine each evening.

The amount of drinking that was going on did begin to alarm some people, and they tried to set limits, not on the drinking itself but on the number of taverns and public houses in which much of the drinking took place. In 1760 John Adams asked the town meeting in Braintree,

Massachusetts, to consider reducing the number of public houses. Adams was ridiculed and his proposal overwhelmingly voted down.

John Adams was the most abstemious of the Founding Fathers, but even he regularly drank a tankard of hard cider with breakfast every morning. Hard cider has about twice the alcoholic content of beer. George Washington was, among other things, a whiskey distiller; Thomas Jefferson had one of the first vineyards in America, and he customarily drank three glasses of wine a day.

The British claimed, with considerable justification, that the American Revolution was hatched in taverns. The common men met in the taverns to toast freedom, organize a militia, and plot their revolution. The Tory aristocrats, who did their drinking at home, condemned the taverns as public nuisances and called those who frequented them drunken and seditious scum.

The success of the Revolution resulted in a temporary increase in the prestige of the tavern and the collapse of any serious efforts to control drinking. Among those freedoms Americans felt they had won was the freedom to drink just as much as they wanted of whatever they wanted, whenever and however they wanted. In 1794 an attempt to enforce a tax on whiskey led to a serious revolt against the new American government in western Pennsylvania. Though the revolt, called the Whiskey Rebellion, was put down by federal troops, it left a legacy of bitterness and was a dramatic indication of just how seriously many Americans took their whiskey as a source of revenue, and as a symbol of individual liberty.

After the Revolution the consumption of alcohol in the United States began to rise, and it rose steadily throughout the first half of the nineteenth century. In his study of drinking in early America, *The Alcoholic Republic*, historian William J. Rorabaugh wrote the following:

> Alcohol was pervasive in American society; it crossed regional, sexual, racial and class lines. Americans drank at home and abroad, alone and together, at work and at play, in fun and in earnest. They drank from the crack of dawn to the crack of dawn. At nights taverns were filled with boisterous, mirth-making tipplers. Americans drank before meals, with meals and after meals. They drank while working in the fields and while traveling across half a continent. They drank in their youth, and, if they lived long enough, in their old age. They drank at formal events, such as weddings, ministerial ordinations, and wakes, and on no occasion. . . .
> Early nineteenth-century America may not have been "a nation of drunkards," but Americans were certainly enjoying a spectacular binge.

There was no such thing as an eighteen- or twenty-one-year-old drinking age. Indeed such an idea would have seemed absurd to nineteenth-century Americans. "I have frequently seen Fathers," wrote one traveler, "wake their Child of a year old from a sound sleep to make it drink Rum or Brandy." American parents began trying to accustom their children to drinking practically from infancy, at least partly in the hope that this would protect them from becoming drunkards later on.

"It is no uncommon thing," wrote one man, "to see a boy of twelve or fourteen years old . . . walk into a tavern in the forenoon to take a glass of brandy and bitters. . . ."

Fathers were proud when their sons could drink with them as equals.

It was considered improper for women to frequent taverns, so they drank at home, and those who regarded ordinary spirits as vulgar had recourse to a variety of highly alcoholic "tonics" and "elixirs." Such concoctions were allegedly medicinal, and thus could be drunk without guilt or shame.

There are many reasons for America's heavy drinking, particularly the drinking of highly alcoholic spirits like rum and whiskey. An obvious one is that the spirits were readily available and comparatively cheap. Rum was made from the sugarcane grown in the West Indies. Before the American Revolution vast quantities of molasses were shipped northwest to the colonies where the substance was distilled into rum. A better grade of rum was made right in the West Indies and sent to thirsty colonists. Rum was practically a medium of international exchange in the Western Hemisphere.

During the Revolution trade between the thirteen colonies and the still British West Indies was disrupted, and cheap rum was no longer easily available. But American farmers were producing a surplus of grain that could be distilled into whiskey. It was much cheaper for farmers to store and transport their grain crops as whiskey. And so whiskey replaced rum as the one drink of choice for most Americans.

Americans often drank spirits because there was really nothing else to drink. There were no soft drinks or bottled fruit juices. Without refrigeration, milk spoiled quickly. Diseases were also transmitted through milk. Abraham Lincoln's mother died from drinking milk from a cow that had eaten poisonous jimson weed.

Water supplies were unreliable, and as a drink, water

was often a bad joke. Of water, said one American, "It's very good for navigation." The aristocratic John Randolph of Virginia warned his son about drinking water. "I see by the papers, eight deaths in one week, in Philadelphia alone," he wrote in 1813. Randolph noted that he never used water when mixing his mint juleps. Benjamin Franklin joked that if God had intended man to drink water, "He would not have made him with an elbow capable of raising a wine glass."

The water supplies really were awful, and the image of a pre-industrial America of clear streams and unpolluted wells is a false one. In St. Louis the drinking water came from the Mississippi, but before people could drink it, they had to allow it to "settle," and the sediment often filled a quarter of the container. Rainwater was better, but during dry seasons there simply wasn't enough of it. Tea was expensive and unpopular. It was associated with England, and many Americans considered it downright unpatriotic to drink the stuff. Coffee was more expensive than whiskey.

Besides, water was tasteless and had no food value. Whiskey, which has some 80 calories per ounce, could and did provide a substantial part of an American's daily food requirement, though it certainly did not provide a balanced diet.

Cider, which was pressed from apples and allowed to ferment, was a very popular drink in areas where apples were grown, but it was bulky and did not travel well. In the early nineteenth century, American beer was bitter, expensive, and hard to ship.

The American diet, particularly on the frontier, was usually monotonous and extremely greasy. The flavor of whiskey helped to overcome the monotony, and the alcohol cut the grease. With such fare it is hardly surprising that Americans hurried through their food in order to get to the tavern for a few hours of leisurely drinking. Americans were puzzled by the European habit of eating slowly, as if they actually enjoyed their food.

The attitude of many Americans was expressed in a bit of doggerel sung to the tune of "Home, Sweet Home":

Mid plenty of bacon and bread tho' we jog
Be it ever so strong, there's nothing like grog.
A shot from the jug sends such joy to the heart,
No eating on earth could such pleasure impart.
Grog, grog, sweet, sweet grog.
There's nothing like grog, there's nothing like grog.

Bolting heavy, greasy, ill-prepared foods produced a typical American malady—indigestion. And for that, as for many other complaints, Americans had one cure—more whiskey.

So Americans drank because the liquor was available, because they liked the taste of the stuff, and because they thought it was good for them; but they also drank quite simply to get drunk.

The greatest drinking holiday in nineteenth-century America was the Fourth of July. People equated independence from England with the independence of drunkenness. It was a "day of national intoxication." Another day upon which Americans drank freely was election day. This was a custom carried over from colonial times. In 1758, when George Washington stood for the House of Burgesses in Virginia, he expressed some anxiety that his election agent had not spent freely enough on liquor for the voters. He had some cause for concern, for he had lost an earlier election to a candidate who had provided drink more generously to the voters. Washington won in

1758 after giving out 144 gallons of rum, punch, wine, and hard cider. His vote total was 307, an investment of about half a gallon per vote.

The candidate not only had to hand out liquor to the voters, he usually had to drink with them, to show that he too was one of the boys, not an arrogant, standoffish aristocrat.

While everyone from ministers to coal miners drank, certain groups drank more than others; lumberjacks and boatmen, for example. Trappers had a peculiarly American drinking pattern. For most of the year they roamed the wilderness alone and sober, for there was no way to get whiskey in the wilderness. But for a few days in the summer of each year the fur-trading companies would host a rendezvous of traders where they could sell their furs, swap stories, gamble, and drink. Oh, how they drank! The rendezvous invariably turned into a drunken revel where a trapper might spend all he had earned during a year of hard and lonely work in just a few days. The fur companies not only bought the pelts, they also sold the whiskey, at great profit. "Spree" or "binge" drinking of this type was also common among sailors, though they usually had a "rum ration" during voyages.

Whiskey was a favorite trade item with the American Indians. For the American Indians, whose entire culture was already under great stress, the introduction of liquor was a disaster of major proportions. Liquor was often used quite cynically, though effectively, by white traders and Indian agents to control the Indians and their land. The tragic legacy of this policy is still evident, for alcoholism remains a major problem for American Indians.

College students were among the lustiest of drinkers. Historian Rorabaugh wrote that the heavy drinking was due in part to stress of change that the students encountered. Colleges in America had been set up primarily to train an elite minority and to produce clergymen. But there were no longer a sufficient number of ministerial positions available, and the elitism conflicted sharply with the new democratic spirit. "Students steeped in ideals of liberty and equality had contempt for institutions whose outmoded curriculums, old-fashioned teachers, and predilection for training clergymen were survivals from colonial times," wrote Rorabaugh.

Whatever their reasons, "This post Revolutionary generation of students indulged in unprecedented lusty drinking," according to Rorabaugh. The drinking was combined with gambling, swearing, licentious behavior, and occasional violence toward the college itself. At Princeton students set fire to the main college hall. It was, Rorabaugh wrote, the students' way of showing contempt for institutions that they no longer respected. The colleges responded first by trying to limit drinking and then by banning it altogether. By 1800 the drinking of spirits was officially banned on most colleges. The regulations, however, were simply ignored.

THE ANTIDRINKING CRUSADE

As the consumption of alcohol went up, opposition to drinking began to revive and grow stronger. Of the religious groups, the Quakers were the first to strongly oppose drinking. Drinking was not only discouraged among Quakers themselves, they were not to engage in the liquor trade and were to be very sparing in their use of liquor as a medicine.

As early as the 1780s the Quakers were joined by the Methodists in their condemnation of distilled spirits. The Baptists, Presbyterians, and other more traditional Protestant denominations were far slower in adopting anti-drinking postures.

It wasn't just the religious leaders who began to look askance at drinking. Mercantile capitalists began to oppose drinking for very practical reasons. In a slower moving agrarian society, drunkenness might be tolerated. If the trapper or sailor went out on an occasional "spree," that did not interfere with his work. A drunken clerk, however, was of little use. A worker in the mills and factories that were being spawned by the Industrial Revolution could not be drunk on the job without slowing down the entire operation, as well as risking death or serious injury to himself and others. Long layoffs for a drinking bout and the necessary recovery time did not fit into the new more efficient system of work. The time spent in passing the jug around or simply standing round after round of drinks was no longer available to the workman. Heavy drinking meant waste and loss of profit. Drinking, which promised immediate gratification, conflicted with the new work ethic, which required delayed gratification or the gratification that came from hard work alone.

In England, where industrialization came earlier than it did to the United States, there were also vigorous efforts to curb the drinking of the "lower orders." There is something almost insufferably pompous and condescending about much of the early antidrinking propaganda. There were lectures to the poor and the working class about the evils of drink, delivered at the behest of the wealthy who were free to drink whatever they wished whenever they chose. Despite the tone, however, there was a good deal of truth in the lectures. A rich drunkard could continue to drink until his liver gave out. A poor drunkard faced quick ruin for himself and his family.

All manner of techniques were tried to get the workingman to stop drinking, or at least to drink less. The antidrink crusaders realized that drinking was central to the social life of the British workingman, that the public house, or pub, was not only where he did his drinking but where he met his friends and spent most of his leisure time. In the nineteenth century there was a well-financed movement to establish workingmen's coffee houses, places where the ordinary pubgoer could get the atmosphere and some of the services of the pub, without the alcohol. Though well financed and enthusiastically supported, this movement was a complete flop. The reasons for the failure were varied but, as popular historian Mark Girouard wrote, "In spite of what the propaganda would lead one to expect, their [the coffee houses'] tea, coffee and food were frequently disgusting, and the surroundings they provided were gloomy and squalid enough to be compared to a 'workhouse dining-hall.'"

"More important," continued Girouard, "in spite of many good resolutions not to patronize or preach to the clientele, their well meaning sponsors were seldom able to refrain from doing both." The interior of these coffee houses were commonly decorated with signs which proclaimed "No drunkard shall inherit the kingdom of God" and "The coming of the Lord draweth nigh." Girouard noted that this "was not a form of decoration calculated to attract independent working men looking for an agreeable meeting place."

The attack on excessive drinking came from yet another source, the medical community, though in early America doctors had been considered among the heartiest of drinkers. Early in the nineteenth century, Dr. David Hosack of New York estimated that in his city 40 of 100 physicians were drunkards. Most people, including doctors, in post-Revolutionary America regarded heavy drinking as not particularly harmful, and in many ways beneficial. There were, however, medical dissenters. As early as 1789 Dr. Benjamin Rush, who had been surgeon general of the Continental Middle Army, wrote an excellent pamphlet on the dangers of "Spiritous Liquors." Dr. Rush, who was unusually well educated for an American physician of that time, had observed the devastating effects of heavy drinking on the men of the Continental Army. He suggested that rum and whiskey be replaced with beer, light wine, weak rum punch, or other, nonalcoholic drinks. Rush did not call for total abstinence but for moderation, for temperance. Dr. Rush's pamphlet was widely circulated, and he received much praise as well as some criticism for it. But while Rush's views were widely known, they were not widely heeded, and drinking to excess went on just as before. Rush was discouraged, and ultimately he came to believe that only religion could cure America's taste for strong drink.

However, around 1840 the drinking habits of Americans began to change, and the overall consumption of alcohol in all forms started dropping sharply, until by the last quarter of the century Americans were drinking only about half as much per person as they had during the first quarter of the century. While the rate of drinking has fluctuated a bit over the last century, it has remained relatively stable. Drinking has not disappeared as the antidrink crusaders once hoped it would, but it has never risen to the whiskey-soaked levels of the early days of the Republic either.

The reasons for the rapid and permanent decline in heavy drinking among Americans are complex and, like most mass changes in behavior, are not really understood. Certainly the exhortations of medical men like Rush as to the dangers of heavy drinking must have had their effect. There seemed to be a general realization that drinking in the United States had simply gotten out of hand.

FROM MODERATION TO ABSTINENCE

Though many religious groups had been slow to throw themselves into the antiliquor crusade, once they took up the cause, they did so with almost fanatical zeal. In nineteenth-century America it was impossible to escape the exhortations of temperance preachers. By this time temperance, which once meant moderation, had come to mean total abstinence from all alcoholic beverages, including those such as beer and wine, which men like Dr. Rush had originally approved. Temperance tracts with their horrifying tales of the evils of liquor were everywhere, and a person could hardly walk down the street without having one thrust into his hand. Every Sunday from a thousand pulpits preachers thundered denunciations of Demon Rum. The "Jolly Toaper" had become "the drunkard," a figure of shame, a man who brought ruin to himself and his family and who posed a threat to society at large. Each city and town had its temperance society, and members engaged in activities from trying to limit the number of saloons to, as in the case of the hatchet-wielding Carrie Nation, actually busting up saloons. Women who saw drunkenness as a threat to family life were prominent in the antidrink movement.

The primary reason for the change in drinking habits may have been the vast social changes that were taking place in the United States. The country had become more stable and more industrial, and while there was still plenty of frontier, the majority of Americans no longer lived on it. They lived in cities, towns, and well-established farming communities. The rootlessness that so often led to heavy drinking was no longer as common.

State and local governments attempted to limit drinking both by restrictive licensing of the places that sold liquor and by heavy taxation of alcoholic beverages, thus making them more expensive, as well as raising revenue. A tax on liquor, then as now, was looked on as a "moral" tax or a "good" tax.

However, for all the success of the antidrinking crusade, and that success was considerable, drinking still did not disappear. Since temperance had become a full-blown moral crusade, partial success was not enough. Liquor was diabolical, and there could be no compromise with the devil. In the days before the Civil War many of those involved in the antidrinking movement were also involved in antislavery movements—yet they regarded drinking and not slavery as the greatest evil. Slaves, they argued, had only lost control of their bodies, while drunkards lost their souls. The chains of intoxication, declared one enthusiastic reformer, "are heavier than those which the sons of Africa have ever worn."

Powerful groups like the Woman's Christian Temperance Union, founded in 1874, and the Anti-Saloon League, founded in 1893, began to push for a total ban on the sale of alcoholic beverages in the United States. Between 1880 and 1900, prohibition laws were passed in Iowa, Kansas, and the Dakotas. By the time World War I ended in 1918, Congress had already submitted the Eighteenth Amendment to the states for ratification. The amendment in effect banned the manufacture, transportation, and sale of all alcoholic beverages. It was ratified by the states with astonishing speed and became effective on January 16, 1920. After that date no one in the United States could get a legal glass of beer or wine, much less a shot of whiskey.

Prohibition was the crowning success of a century of antidrinking agitation in the United States. But other less admirable sentiments also contributed to the success of the prohibition movement, notably an antiforeign and particularly an anti-Catholic bias. The early twentieth century saw an unprecedented wave of immigration to the United States. Many of these new immigrants were Catholics, and the Protestant majority felt threatened. Since the antidrinking crusade was led by Protestant clergymen and not notably supported by the Catholic newcomers, the hatred of liquor and fear of Catholics with their "foreign drinking habits" were combined. There was also a political edge to Prohibition. Republicans were more generally supporters of Prohibition and thus were considered the "drys," while Democrats were more likely to be hostile and thus were the "wets." The attitude was neatly summed up by one preacher who at a Republican rally denounced the Democrats as the party of "Rum, Romanism and Rebellion."

The triumph of Prohibition ironically proved to be the greatest disaster that the antidrinking forces had ever suffered, for the ban proved to be virtually unenforceable. Prohibition was a spectacular and immediate failure, the most dramatic example in American history of the proposition that morality cannot be legislated.

Those who were allied with the temperance movement didn't drink anyway, and the public in general did not regard drinking as either a mortal sin or a crime. President Warren Harding, in office during Prohibition, was a notable drinker and kept a well-stocked bar in the White House. He just didn't drink in public.

Illegal liquor flowed freely from many sources. Making beer and liquor is not that difficult, so "home brew" and "bathtub gin" became standard drinks. A local "moonshiner" might only distill enough for his neighbors. An illegal brewery could supply an entire city or region.

Many of these drinks could be vile tasting or downright dangerous. But the tales of people who had been sickened or killed by compounds that turned out to be poisonous did little to discourage drinking of illegally manufactured liquor and beer.

During the early days of Prohibition, heavily alcoholic "medicinal compounds" were available over the counter, but the government quickly cracked down on that obvious ruse. Some liquor was legally dispensed by doctor's prescription, and some doctors were extraordinarily generous in writing prescriptions.

America was trying to be a "dry" island in a wet world, and it was impossible. Liquor was still made and sold legally in Canada (though there were some liquor restrictions after World War I) and the West Indies. Smuggling and rum running became profitable enterprises.

The illegal trade in alcoholic beverages became big business, and this business was controlled by crime figures who became more powerful than they had ever been before. The whole structure of organized crime, which still plagues the United States today, was established during the Prohibition era.

The vast illegal liquor trade could never have survived without the active cooperation of a large percentage of the political and law enforcement officials of the nation. With bootlegging as a multimillion-dollar business, there was always plenty of money around to pay off those who were supposed to be enforcing the law. Prohibition stimulated corruption. From time to time there were raids, and speakeasies were closed down and stills broken up. It hardly made a dent in the business.

Most significantly, the illegal liquor trade could not have flourished without the support of the public. People wanted to drink, they didn't think there was anything wrong with drinking, and so they didn't really care where the liquor came from. Although Prohibition did make drinking more difficult and sometimes more dangerous, it certainly didn't stop drinking. Moreover, it spawned widespread disrespect for the law.

The "noble experiment," as Prohibition has been called, was an ignoble failure; in 1933 the Constitution had been amended once again, this time to repeal national Prohibition. What was left was a confusing patchwork of state and local laws and regulations concerning the sale of alcoholic beverages. Some counties and even states remained "dry." Some areas did not allow the sale of liquor by the drink, others have all liquor sold through state-operated stores. In some areas beer, wine, and liquor can be sold in supermarkets and variety stores that are open seven days a week. Taxes vary greatly, and so does the age at which people are allowed to drink legally.

But there is now a serious attempt to raise the drinking age in all states to twenty-one, and that is a legal change that will affect you most directly.

9

You Can Vote, But You Can't Drink

FOUR TEENS KILLED IN CRASH

Headlines like that scream out at you with alarming regularity. As you read down through the story there is often a phrase which says that the police believe that the accident was "alcohol related." What the story means is that some kid who had too much to drink got into the car and killed himself and some friends who happened to be riding with him. A variation is the kid driving home from a party who plows into another car and escapes without a scratch, but who kills or seriously injures the people in the other car who were obeying all the laws.

Drunken driving is a subject that is very much on people's minds today. It's a problem everyone says we should "do something" about.

Despite all the interest and all the studies on drunk driving and the best way to curb it, the facts are not nearly as clear and unambiguous as most of those who talk about the subject would have us believe. For example, the incidence of alcohol-related traffic accidents does not appear to be significantly higher now than it was say ten years ago. But public attitudes toward drunk driving have changed significantly. A number of highly effective citizens' groups have been formed to push for tougher laws. There is a great deal of public pressure to enforce current laws more strictly. A decade ago drunk driving was thought of as a fact of modern life that couldn't be altered. Not anymore. Now it is regarded as a crime, and one that should be punished severely.

However, the changes that are being brought about by this new public awareness of drunk driving are not going to affect all segments of the population equally. You are going to shoulder the heaviest part of the burden—whether you deserve it or not. Though there is some talk of drunk driving being a problem for people of all ages, in general adults perceive the problem of drunk driving and teen drinking as identical. The major legal change to come out of the concern over drunk driving is a general lifting of the age that one can legally drink to twenty-one.

As we noted in the last chapter, the end of Prohibition left the United States with a patchwork of laws and regulations governing the sale of alcohol. In some states the legal age was as low as eighteen, but in the majority it was twenty-one. During the 1960s and early 1970s there was a general movement in the country toward greater rights and freedoms for young people. A constitutional amendment allowing eighteen-year-olds to vote in national elections was finally passed. There was also the war in Vietnam, where a lot of eighteen-year-olds were being sent out to fight and possibly die for their country.

The slogan became, "Old enough to vote, or old enough to fight, then old enough to drink." In the early 1970s about thirty states lowered the age at which their citizens could legally buy alcoholic beverages. Now that trend has been dramatically and forcefully reversed. What's happened? A number of things.

It's now been over fifty years since the disastrous experiment with Prohibition ended. There are relatively few still alive who clearly recall the bathtub gin, gang wars, and general disrespect for the law that the era spawned. Regulating drinking has become a more acceptable idea.

Some citizens' groups, particularly Mothers Against Drunk Driving (MADD), have been extremely effective in making the public aware of the terrifying human cost of drunk driving. The chilling statistic of an estimated 25,000 alcohol-related highway deaths a year has finally begun to sink in. The campaigns have made people realize that drunk driving is not just an individual problem. Drunk drivers risk their own lives, but they also risk the lives of everyone else in the car and everyone else on the highway. If drunk driving is a societywide problem, then society must try to deal with it. Moreover, people have begun to feel that society can do something about drunk driving, that it's not just an unalterable fact of modern life like crowded highways.

Concern over drug use, particularly among teens, forced many adults to begin thinking about their own drinking habits. Their kids would ask, why are you getting so upset over a little pot when you drink a couple of martinis or a half a dozen beers a day? It is not an easy or comfortable question to answer.

No one can seriously argue with the genuine concern over the massive problems created by alcohol abuse in this country, particularly the problems of drunk driving. The alcoholic can kill himself and destroy his family—that's awful enough—but the drunk driver can kill you if you just happen to be in the wrong place at the wrong time—that's even worse.

But you're probably saying to yourself, "Why me? Why do people my age always get blamed? Old man Bronson down the block gets loaded every Friday night after work and drives home fifteen miles from his favorite bar. Nobody's going to take away his right to buy a drink. The Martinsons have parties for their friends every month. Sometimes the people leaving the party can barely walk— but they drive home. There's no law against serving alcohol at their parties."

It's not fair, you say, it's discriminatory. If that's what you believe, you could make a good case for your position. Even some of those who are actively trying to get the drinking age raised will admit privately that such a move is unfair and discriminatory.

Indeed, there is an unpleasant and worrisome side to the entire campaign to raise the drinking age. It is the most visible and effective edge of a movement that has been called neotemperance or the new Prohibitionism. Practically everyone will say they're not against responsible drinking, they're just against drunk driving or alcohol abuse. However, for many people, just beneath the surface there lurks the old Demon Rum. For them alcohol is not a practical problem or a medical problem—it's a moral problem. Prohibition was repealed, but the type of thinking that was once powerful enough to sway the nation has not really disappeared.

Let's look a bit more closely at the campaign against drunk driving. The problem has two parts—drinking and the driving. Hard liquor ads are banned from television, and in beer and wine ads you can't actually show anyone drinking. (If an intelligent being from another planet had to judge human behavior solely by looking at TV ads, the alien would conclude that beer was a liquid that was often poured but never drunk.) Now there is a move to ban even this advertising on the grounds that it makes drinking look too attractive to young people. True enough.

However, there is no move to ban automobile advertising that makes fast and even reckless driving look attractive to young people. Just watch a few of those car commercials on TV tonight and you'll see what we mean. Speed is also a factor in the majority of fatal auto accidents.

How about those thrilling car chases in teen films? Don't they encourage wild driving? What about auto racing which, even with all the safety precautions, really is a dangerous activity? Oh sure, all the drivers will tell you that you shouldn't drive this way on the street, but isn't the excitement and glamour that surrounds the Indy 500 just as likely to encourage a young person to drive too fast, as the sight of a couple of paunchy former athletes boosting beer is likely to encourage a young person to drink too much? Many race cars are backed by beer companies, which have their brand name plastered all over the car.

We're not trying to build a case for banning auto racing or for keeping beer commercials on TV; we're merely trying to point up the different attitudes toward drinking and driving—driving is moral, drinking ain't.

The freedoms that young people took or were granted during the 1960s and early 1970s have created resentment and an adult backlash. There has been a general move to tighten up the restrictions on young people. School discipline, not student rights, is the big issue in education today. A back-to-basics movement in many schools really means more rote learning, less scope for independent thinking. Some schools, with parental approval, have instituted searches that would be unconstitutional outside of a school. Others have brought in undercover police to ferret out possible drug dealing. Adults are rarely subjected to that sort of treatment.

The move to raise the drinking age fits neatly with the nostalgic belief on the part of many adults that in "my day" kids didn't do those sorts of things, and the world would be a better place if kids just "obeyed." Combine that with the feeling that drinking is immoral and you have a very potent psychological mixture indeed.

Certainly not everybody who wants the drinking age raised has an ulterior or unconscious motive. Many adults genuinely perceive a hike in the drinking age to twenty-one as an effective way to attack a horrible problem—the staggering number of teens who are killed or maimed every year in alcohol-related traffic accidents.

Even in the area of traffic accidents, statistics are not nearly as solid as you might expect. And, as we shall see, there are lots of ways to interpret the statistics. But a couple of statistics are very clear indeed. Drivers under twenty-one are involved in much more than their share of serious traffic accidents. A lot of teens die as the result of drinking and driving. Those are hard facts that cannot be ignored.

Yes, we know you think that you're a better driver than most older folks. You've got more stamina and much better reflexes. You're sure you can do things on the road that older people just can't do. You're probably quite right.

But being young gives you more than good reflexes, it also gives most of you a confidence, a willingness to take risks, a recklessness that older people lose. That daring is one of the things that makes being young so wonderful and so important. Changes in everything from politics to science are often made by the young who are willing to take risks. If we were all born with the mentality of a forty-year-old, the human race would never have progressed. We would always be listening to those voices which say, "it can't be done, so don't try it." We would still be back there in the caves, afraid to try anything new, afraid to take a risk.

Behind the wheel of a car, however, this wonderful willingness to take risks often leads to trying things that shouldn't or can't be done, like cornering at 60 mph in your beatup old car with the bald tires or trying to drive a hundred miles to see your girlfriend when you only had three hours of sleep the previous night and are dozing off behind the wheel.

Add a few drinks and the danger increases dramatically. Just a beer or two can slow your reflexes and dull your perceptions. Not a lot. If you were walking down the street no one would think you were drunk. Perhaps no one would guess that you had a drink. You might pass a breathalyzer or blood alcohol test. But the slight change brought about by a drink or two might be just enough to have you make a critical, perhaps fatal mistake if you normally take chances while you are driving.

In addition to the physical effect of the alcohol, it also has a psychological effect. You know that a drink or two can make you feel great, on top of the world. It can change you from a tongue-tied clod to a fellow who can talk with ease to anyone. It can also make you feel as if you can pass that car up ahead, when cold sober you would have doubted you could make it, and probably wouldn't try. You are more likely to try and pass that car when there are three other guys in your car who have also been drinking, and they're all yelling, "Go for it!"

Drinking also makes you sleepy. When coming home from a late party with a few drinks under your belt it's oh-so-easy to doze off and wake up in a ditch, or much worse.

Drinking and driving for teens can be a very serious

problem. But is raising the drinking age to twenty-one the best solution? It certainly isn't a fair solution. In the first place, it discriminates against young women. You might notice that in the previous examples we always said *he*. That was deliberate, for women under the age of twenty-one do not have an exceptionally large number of alcohol-related accidents. Indeed, statistically they are among the safest of drivers. On the other hand some statistics indicate that men between the ages of twenty-one and twenty-four are the ones most likely to get drunk and have an auto accident, even in areas where it is legal for eighteen-year-olds to drink. So what's the answer, raise the drinking age to twenty-four or even thirty-four because men between twenty-five and thirty-four have more than their share of alcohol-related accidents as well? That's not likely to happen. When faced with a problem, society usually tries to solve it by dumping it on the most powerless group—and that's you.

As we noted, some honest proponents of the twenty-one-year-old drinking age will admit that it's unfair and discriminatory and that there is no good response to the query, if you're old enough to vote, aren't you old enough to drink? Some have the uncomfortable feeling that the campaign is a cop-out that does not attack the real problem of drinking and driving, and that once the drinking age is raised, people will assume the problem is solved and will ignore it. However, uncomfortable or not, most say raising the drinking age will save lives—and that's the bottom line.

But does it? In the early 1970s when states lowered the drinking age, there was a jump in the number of alcohol-related accidents and deaths among teens. In the mid-1970s, when many states began raising their drinking ages again, they reported a decrease in the number of alcohol-related traffic accidents and deaths among teens. But was this decrease due to the new restrictions or to the fact that the total number of teens was beginning to fall after the mid-1970s? The statistics are not absolutely clear on this point. And even if the decrease was due to the higher drinking age, how long would it last? A lot of publicity and a concentrated effort by the police might change drinking and driving habits for a while. But forced changes are rarely permanent. Campaigns in the media fall off. The police turn their attention to other matters. And you know that if you're under age and you want a drink, you won't have much trouble getting it, no matter what the law says. In a few years we may discover that a change in the drinking age has no significant effect on teen drinking and driving.

Some researchers say that there is even a real possibility that in the long run raising the drinking age will actually increase the number of alcohol-related accidents among teens. If kids can't drink legally in bars or clubs where there is at least some supervision, then they will find other settings in which they can drink, for example, riding around in their cars, or parked in some remote spot where they are less likely to be caught. The authors, who grew up at a time when most states had a twenty-one-year-old drinking age, can testify that car drinking was common. Settings like that increase drinking and driving. There is evidence to indicate that in areas where there are a lot of rigidly enforced rules against drinking, total drinking may be less common, but there is more drunkenness and there are more alcohol-related accidents. The National Institute on Alcohol Abuse and Alcoholism says, "Alcoholism and problem drinking rates tend to be low among groups whose drinking habits are well integrated with the rest of their culture."

Some colleges have established bars and pubs on campus so students don't have to drive to get a drink. If the drinking age is raised, these places will close and students will start driving to places where they can drink. This, some college officials feel, increases the danger of drinking and driving.

So raising the drinking age is not fair. It may not even be effective in cutting down the number of accidents. But if the state you're living in hasn't raised its drinking age yet, it probably will shortly. At the time of this writing some twenty states have already raised their legal drinking ages, and the push is on to establish a national legal drinking age of twenty-one. In New York State a Democratic governor who is a leading spokesman for liberal causes in the country is spearheading the fight to raise the drinking age. Nationally a law mandating a cut in federal highway funds to states that have not raised their drinking age has been signed by a conservative Republican president who had always insisted that the federal government should not interfere in the actions of the states. The push for twenty-one is a powerful and broad-based one. At this moment in history the tide may well be irresistible.

If you feel that you are being discriminated against simply because you are young, what can you do? Well, you can bring the subject up for discussion in your school. You can write your state legislators. You can even get up a delegation to see your legislators. Frankly, we can't hold out much hope for success. Just recently a group of high school students who tried to talk to legislators on the subject was dismissed, quite contemptuously, as simply participating in a "civics lesson." Other legislators might be smoother or more polite, but they won't listen either. You haven't got much clout on this subject. Twenty-one, like motherhood, is a popular issue with most voters who happen to be over twenty-one and won't be personally affected anymore.

The organized tavern owners who will be affected are fighting twenty-one, sometimes quite successfully, but they have their own reasons.

So you can grind your teeth and rail against the injustice of the world, but it's a world you have to live in. The first thing you must do is be realistic. If you drink, the chances are that you are already drinking illegally. The cops are not going to bust into your house and grab you because you've had a few beers. They are not likely to raid orderly parties looking for illegal booze, as they might if they suspected drugs were around. Even if you are caught trying to buy liquor illegally, you probably will not be in really big trouble. If you are caught drunk while driving, however, then you are in double trouble. *So don't do it.*

But do you really need laws and the fear of losing your driver's license and possibly going to jail to keep you from drinking and driving? You shouldn't. You shouldn't even need statistics about the number of alcohol-related auto accidents every year. All you have to do is look around you. We'll bet that you know someone just about your own age who has been seriously injured or killed in an auto accident where drinking was involved. Maybe you've been in an accident yourself or you've had a close call. Next time you could be the one seriously injured or killed.

So forget all the statistics, all the arguments, all the laws. Just remember that drinking and driving is like playing Russian roulette and that one little mistake can change your life, or end it, for alcohol-related traffic accidents are a leading, perhaps the leading, cause of death among teens.

10

What's a Drinking Problem?

Alcohol is something that most people can take or leave alone. But there are those who can't leave it alone, even when they should.

CRAIG

Craig, eighteen, was finding his senior year really rough. It was supposed to be the best year of his life, but so far it had been nothing but trouble. His grades were good, good enough to get him into honor society. He had been on the swim team for three years. Girls seemed to find him good-looking. On the surface things were going well. He was a success.

Craig's parents were doctors, the family had plenty of money, and he seemed to have "everything"—a car, vacations in Europe, the latest stereo and video camera. Of course, he lived in a beautiful suburban house. But if Craig's parents gave him the best, they expected the best from him. In their view he was destined for an Ivy League college and a career in medicine, law, high tech, something worthy of all the advantages they had given him.

Still, they knew better than to "spoil" Craig, and the summer before his senior year he worked for a landscaper.

Doing manual labor gave Craig plenty of time to think. The realization that he had one year left before he went off to college and his life changed completely hit him hard. He was terrified of the future, afraid that he wouldn't be able to live up to everybody's expectations. Craig had done his share of drinking at parties. Everybody in his crowd drank. But now he found that an occasional drink in the morning calmed him and made it possible for him to go to work and cope with his fears. When he tried to talk to his parents about his anxieties, he was met by a wall of unrealistic optimism, reassurances that didn't reassure. His parents refused to take his concerns seriously.

Craig's boss was hard to get along with, and one day in early August when Craig felt he was being singled out and picked on, he lost his temper and told his boss exactly what he thought. That outburst got him fired on the spot. This was a major crisis for Craig, who was used to being praised. His parents were calm when he told them what happened, but they didn't accept his view of the situation. He sensed an undercurrent of icy coldness and only wished his parents could admit they were disappointed in him. He was disappointed in himself.

Craig was home alone the rest of the summer. His friends were busy, and it was too late to find another job. To kill the boredom and the anxiety, he drank. Though he told himself he was drinking too much, he didn't really feel strong enough to stop. The expensive bottles of scotch lining his parents' liquor cabinet were too tempting. They were his best companions during the long empty days.

Fall came and with it the dreaded senior year. He would have to retake the SATs because the first time his scores had been only good; this time they had better be spectacular. There would be interviews and visits to colleges, application forms, essays to write, farewells to be said at the end of the year. Craig found the time between drinks harder to bear. He kept a thermos of whiskey in his locker to cut the waiting time down.

Friends noticed that he wasn't very friendly anymore. He was forever coming up with excuses to avoid them, pleading homework, a date, anything to stay alone at night and drink. He kept a bottle hidden in his room, and since by now he'd become an agile liar, he always found a reason to slip away to his room where he'd take a few quick gulps.

So far he'd managed to hold things together, to keep up his homework and make it through classes. Then a series of blows made him drink more. Rejections from several prestigious colleges started showing up in the mail. It got so his stomach tightened into knots when he opened the mailbox after school. His father was shocked; his mother enraged. They complained about Ivy League schools. What criteria do they use? What are they looking for? But this didn't help. It only made Craig feel a keen sense of personal failure.

As the year went on and graduation came closer he reached the point where he had to drink first thing in the morning. Often he woke up with a hangover and decided that the only cure was another drink. He'd get up, run the bathwater in his bathroom to drown out the sounds of his throwing up, then return to his room and start drinking. After a while he was ready to rush out of the house, shouting to his mother that he had no time for breakfast because he was late.

But the pretense was wearing thin. He seemed to lose his temper easily these days, getting into fights in school, something that never happened to him before he started drinking. It was hard to concentrate in class, and he would often fall asleep. One of the women who worked in the cafeteria noticed that he skipped lunch regularly. Girls were aware just how much Craig had changed. He'd ask somebody out, then break the date, be hyper-friendly part of the time and cold and preoccupied the next time they met. Rumors circulated at school that he was on drugs.

It was a relief that his parents were so busy, so rarely at home. He wasn't worried about the housekeeper, just as long as she didn't come across a bunch of empty bottles, and he was very careful about that. Sometimes Craig felt guilty about drinking so much, but then he'd remind himself that he was still in control. There were scary moments, of course. There was the time he blacked out and literally couldn't remember anything that had happened to him the night before. And there was the morning he'd accidentally burned himself pouring hot coffee because his hand was unsteady and because he was feeling slightly dizzy.

His appearance was on the downslide, too. He was becoming sloppier, more careless, but he didn't have the energy to concentrate on his clothes or his hair. All his resources were directed toward getting a drink and preventing people from blocking this goal.

Craig is a young man with a serious drinking problem. He could be an alcoholic or, depending on one's definition, well on the road to becoming one.

Did we hear you say, "Here comes the commercial, the warning about the fatal glass of beer." No, not at all. The great majority of people in our society drink, and only a small percentage of the drinkers develop serious problems because of their drinking. But it would be very foolish to deny that serious problems sometimes do arise. In this chapter we will discuss some of the problems.

ALCOHOLISM AND DRUNKENNESS

We must first make a distinction often ignored in discussions of drinking problems—there is a vast difference between alcoholism and drunkenness. Let's take up the subject of alcoholism first.

The person who doesn't like to drink and rarely if ever touches the stuff will almost certainly never become an alcoholic. The guy lying drunk in the gutter with a pint of cheap wine sticking out of the pocket of his ragged coat almost certainly is an alcoholic. Between those two extremes lies a huge area of disagreement and confusion about alcoholism. Despite the fact that alcoholism has been intensively studied for decades, there is no scientific test for it nor indeed any universally accepted definition of the word. Alcoholism is generally regarded as a disease, rather than a moral failing, though an aura of moralizing almost always clings to the subject. Alcoholism is usually defined more by what it does than what it is. One article on the subject says alcoholism is "drinking that infringes on health, job, marriage and friendship or family relationships."

In its definition of alcoholism, the World Health Organization recognizes that different cultures define alcoholism differently and gives this broad definition: "A chronic, behavioral disorder, marked by repeated drinking of alcohol in excess of the dietary and social customs of the community and to an extent that it interferes with the drinker's health or how he functions socially or economically."

The American Medical Association also uses a broad

definition: "Alcoholism is an illness characterized by preoccupation with alcohol and loss of control over its consumption such as to lead usually to intoxication if drinking; by chronicity; by progression; and by a tendency toward relapse. It is typically associated with physical disability and impaired emotional, occupational and/or social adjustment as a direct consequence of persistent excessive use."

The point at which a heavy drinker or even a problem drinker becomes an alcoholic cannot be scientifically determined. It depends on one's definition of alcoholic. In the view of Mrs. Fred Tooze of the National Woman's Christian Temperance Union, an alcoholic is "anyone who drinks alcohol. As soon as they start to drink, they're on that road downward." In a sense that's true, for if you never touch alcohol, you'll never become an alcoholic. But that definition is distinctly an eccentric one, for most people who do drink do not find their lives or health disrupted by alcohol.

Though alcoholics certainly drink a great deal, the amount one drinks is not necessarily a reliable measure of alcoholism. There are heavy drinkers who appear to "handle it" pretty well, and the drinking does not seem to dominate their lives. They are able to stop before they get into serious trouble. There are others who consume less alcohol every day than many heavy drinkers, yet become totally dependent upon it.

Why one drinker becomes an alcoholic and another does not remains a puzzle, despite thousands of scientific studies. The origins of alcoholism seem to lie in a complex mixture of body chemistry, heredity, and social and economic background. Indeed, what is called alcoholism is probably not a single disease or condition at all.

The appearance of being drunk is also not necessarily

a reliable guide to who is and who is not an alcoholic. An individual who gets roaring drunk fairly regularly may not touch a drink between binges. An alcoholic, on the other hand, may be able to drink almost constantly and yet not appear drunk to the casual observer. Thus some alcoholics are able to hide and even deny their problem for many years, although alcoholism is rarely a secret from the members of an alcoholic's immediate family for very long.

Strains of laboratory mice have been bred to become alcoholics—that is, these mice prefer alcohol to water. There is something different about the body chemistry of such mice. These and other studies indicate that there may be a genetic factor in alcoholism.

There is a common belief that alcoholism runs in families, and statistical studies seem to support this belief. But this does not necessarily mean that alcoholism is hereditary. Simply growing up in a household where there is an alcoholic may expose a child to the sort of conditions that trigger alcoholism. Yet studies of the adopted children of alcoholics indicate that even if the child has been adopted at birth and raised in a nonalcoholic environment, he or she has a greater chance of becoming an alcoholic than does the adopted child of nonalcoholic parents raised under similar conditions.

Whereas the evidence is far from solid or overwhelming, it does seem to indicate that there is an inherited genetic predisposition to alcoholism. Does that mean that the children of an alcoholic parent are doomed to alcoholism themselves? Of course not! The majority of children of alcoholics do not become alcoholics themselves. The key word here is *predisposition*. We inherit predispositions to lots of things, including diseases like heart disease and cancer.

On a practical level what this should mean is that if you come from a family where alcoholism has been a problem, it would be wise for you to be more careful about your drinking habits, more aware of potential difficulties, just as a person who comes from a family with a predisposition to heart disease should watch his or her diet more closely.

The type of culture a person lives in influences the development of alcoholism. In some cultures heavy drinking, indeed getting very, very drunk is considered an essential part of having a good time. Masculinity may be closely tied to drinking, with virility being measured, at least in part, by the amount of alcohol one can consume without falling over. The brawling, hard-drinking John Wayne is still the ideal masculine image for many.

The most spectacular display of drunkenness that the authors ever witnessed was at a traditional Scottish New Year's Eve or Hogmanay celebration. Though most of the people at the party were thoroughly respectable, middle-class, and middle-aged, the amount of drinking easily surpassed the wildest of college parties and made the typical alcohol-soaked American New Year's Eve party look like a tea party. Yet no one seemed to feel that the amount of drinking was excessive or unusual—it was simply the traditional way of celebrating. Most of the drinking was done by the men. The women had to stay sober enough to get their husbands home.

Obviously in a social environment that encourages heavy drinking, those individuals who are susceptible to alcoholism are far more likely to succumb. Among the Scots, alcoholism is a big problem. Other cultures do not encourage drunkenness, and alcoholism is less common. In Italy, Italians consume large quantities of wine with meals, but are under no pressure to "get drunk," indeed, drunkenness is frowned upon. Most Jews of Eastern European origin rarely drank any alcoholic beverages, except a little wine on religious holidays or other special occasions.

These cultural differences in drinking habits are not inborn or permanent. Once people have lived in America for a few generations, the sharp distinctions that originally existed between various immigrant groups begin to blur, and people from all backgrounds tend to adopt the drinking habits common to the majority of Americans.

Religion can also influence the amount a person drinks. There are some religious groups, primarily conservative Protestants, where drinking of any kind is actively and strongly discouraged. The sanctions work, and as a result people who belong to such groups generally don't drink or at least don't drink in public. However, rigid antidrinking rules may create problems for a percentage of persons from such backgrounds. Even moderate drinking can result in a person's being rejected and excluded. Set adrift, the individual may drink even more. Drinking may also produce guilt that causes the individual to drink more to drown out the guilt.

Social class is yet another influence on drinking habits. We Americans are often uncomfortable about admitting that there is even such a thing as social class in our country, but of course there is. Studies have shown that in general people who are wealthier and better educated and have higher status jobs tend to drink more than those who are poor and uneducated. However, the same studies indicate that it is among the poor and the poorly educated that drinking creates the most severe problems. The poor man who drinks (for the vast majority of these problems arise among men) is far more likely to lose his job and run afoul of the police. He is also more likely to be labeled an alcoholic than a rich drinker. During times of economic crisis alcoholism and associated problems tend to rise sharply among the poor.

It's reasonable to assume that the stresses created by poverty drive people to seek relief in alcohol. But there are many other personal stresses that can literally drive people to drink. Alcohol can produce temporary euphoria, relaxation, even oblivion, and at moments such escapes may seem desirable or even necessary. In the case of Craig it was the emotional pressure brought about by unrealistically high expectations as well as the uncertainty of facing the transition from high school to college that triggered his drinking problems. Another individual facing exactly the same pressures might react very differently.

So like everything else about alcoholism, its causes are complex and unclear.

We could go on at great length describing the horrors of alcoholism, the emotional and physical deterioration, the pain and terror of withdrawal. But we suspect that you've heard all of that already. If you've ever known an alcoholic, and chances are pretty high that you have, then you've seen how this condition can literally destroy a person's life and the lives of those around him.

We could present scores of conflicting studies on the causes and cures of alcoholism. Though science is supposed to be objective and rational, the study of alcoholism is charged with emotion. The traditional medical view has been that a person who was an alcoholic could never drink again without being in deadly peril of relapsing once again into his former condition. Then in the early 1970s some researchers produced a study that indicated some former alcoholics could and did successfully become moderate drinkers. The results of the study were disputed—that's common in science—but in this case the scientists who did the study were accused of incompetence, even fraud, by other researchers. The whole controversy took on the tone of a religious dispute, not a scientific one. Alcoholism is a subject that even scientists have difficulty approaching rationally and calmly.

YOUR DRINKING BEHAVIOR

We suspect that you really don't want a lengthy rundown on all the medical and psychological experiments and theories about alcoholism. Do you know, for example, that Siamese fighting fish become even more aggressive when alcohol is added to their tankwater? Do you care? What you are interested in are answers to practical and personal questions like: "How about me? Could I become an alcoholic? Are my drinking habits going to lead to trouble? Are any of my friends on their way to becoming alcoholics?"

While alcoholism is generally a condition that develops over a period of years, the teenage alcoholic is not an unknown phenomenon. There are lots of self-tests and quizzes that have been devised to help people spot their own drinking problems. Here is one that was prepared by the federal government.

1. Do you think and talk about drinking often?
2. Do you drink more now than you used to?
3. Do you sometimes gulp drinks?
4. Do you often take a drink to help you relax?
5. Do you drink when you are alone?
6. Do you sometimes forget what happened while you were drinking?
7. Do you keep a bottle hidden somewhere—at home or work—for quick pick-me-ups?
8. Do you need a drink to have fun?

9. Do you ever just start drinking without really thinking about it?
10. Do you drink in the morning to relieve a hangover?

A person who answers yes to four or more of the questions may have a problem, according to those who prepared the quiz. However, this test was designed for adults, and the drinking habits of teens and adults are not necessarily the same. Besides, alcoholism or potential alcoholism cannot be diagnosed on the basis of a simple self-test. Even doctors disagree.

The best way to tell if your drinking habits may be leading to alcoholism is to take a good honest look at yourself. We know that denying the existence of a problem is one of the hallmarks of alcoholism, but if you're going to lie to yourself, then you will lie on a self-test as well.

Ask yourself if drinking has become a big part of your life. Do you find your work at school slipping because you are often too drunk or too hung over to be able to work? Are you missing school for the same reason? Are you spending a lot of money on booze? Can you have a good time without it? Do you find yourself drifting away from old friends and spending more time with "drinking buddies"? Have you begun to become ashamed of or worried about the amount you are drinking?

Every drinker has said to himself or herself, "I can stop anytime I want." Can you? Try it and see.

Are others, old friends, parents, teachers beginning to be concerned about your drinking? They are not necessarily the best judges, but then neither are you. Listen to what they say, because they may be seeing you more clearly than you see yourself.

If you're worried, then it's time to seek out some help. If you can talk honestly with your parents or some other relative, that would be a good place to start. If there is a school counselor or psychologist or a doctor that you feel comfortable with and have confidence in, he or she can be consulted. If religion is important in your life, a sympathetic member of the clergy is another person who might be helpful. In addition, there are organizations that we will list in chapter 13 that may be contacted.

Don't panic! This is very important. There is a difference between the chronic alcoholic and someone who has simply been temporarily drinking too much. Excessive drinking may simply be a response to a particular situation or phase of life. Teens are chronic overreactors. In any case, alcoholism is not an inevitably fatal disease— it's a condition that is completely controllable. The decline can be halted and reversed before permanent damage is done. And that is particularly true for the young. Don't fall for the myth that you have to "hit bottom" before you can be cured. That's just an excuse to put off getting help.

We noted that there is an important distinction to be made between drunkenness and alcoholism, and it is drunkenness that is the big problem for most teen drinkers. Let's look at a typical case.

TODD

Whenever seventeen-year-old Todd came home, his mother would meet him at the door with complaints, requests, and a good chunk of nagging. His four younger brothers and sisters would surround him, adding to the clamor. Todd rarely became angry. He knew that his mother depended on him, and he always turned over part of his paycheck to her. His father was long gone. He'd walked out on the family when Todd was a kid and hadn't been heard from since. Todd was fond of his brothers and sisters. He helped take care of them, worried about them, did what he could for them. But it was tough going to high school, working long hours on a job, and living in a small crowded apartment.

When he was home, he'd have a few beers and watch television. But weekends were party time. Basically Todd was shy and rather uncomfortable with new people or people he didn't know well. Since drinking relaxed him, he'd always drink a lot at parties. He'd clown around, put on a macho act around his friends. Some of the guys he knew had a rock band, and he loved to hang out with them. Parties were always better with music.

At home, life was dead and gray. Parties were full of noise, light, and color. They were getting longer and wilder, and instead of beer, many people he knew had started drinking the hard stuff.

When Todd met his friends at school on Monday, they would reminisce about the last party, show off by telling stories, and compare all the crazy things they'd done. Joe had gone swimming in the river drunk at 3:00 AM. Warren had climbed out on a rock ledge overlooking the valley and threatened to jump off as a joke. Bruce had challenged Paul to a beer-drinking contest, and Todd had gotten so drunk he had fallen down a flight of stairs.

Todd knew a lot of people who didn't drink much, but they weren't nearly as much fun as the people who did. Besides, what could he say to them? Talking about drinking, kidding around about it, planning the next bash— these were what his social life was all about. Lately, he had begun meeting his musician friends in a bar where a lot of musicians hung out. He liked the atmosphere. Even when he'd only have a beer or two he valued the camaraderie, the feeling of belonging. Bars were so much more interesting than the pizza place where a lot of the teens at his school went.

Todd never drank at school or at work, but somehow the day wasn't complete without at least one drink, and, oh, those weekend binges. He really looked forward to them, coming up with excuses to celebrate when no real reason existed. And celebrating was synonymous with drinking. He'd even started drinking early on party nights, and then prolonging the festivities with just one more, one last glass. Somehow the last wasn't quite the last until Todd passed out drunk and had to be dragged home to the endless amusement and wild cheering of his friends.

Whatever else he may be, Todd is certainly not a secret drinker—his drinking and his drunkenness are public, spectacularly so. The sheer bravado of it is part of the fun. By most definitions Todd is no alcoholic. He may be building toward that condition later in life, but maybe not. The drinking may otherwise damage his health some years down the road. But there is a more immediate problem. Simply being that drunk that often carries great risks.

There is the chance of getting sick and the near inevitability of suffering a whopping hangover. But there is also the chance of doing something dangerously stupid. Drinking lowers inhibitions and clouds judgment. Todd and his friends found some of their drunken stunts wonderfully funny. They wouldn't have been at all funny if someone had been injured or killed. The greatest danger a teen faces when he has been drinking is when he gets behind the wheel of a car, but a huge number of other accidents from accidental drownings to falling down the stairs happen to a person when he or she is drunk. Studies have shown that over half the drowning victims have been drinking. About one-quarter of those who suffer severe household accidents had been drinking.

Todd is a "good drunk"—that is, when drunk he tends to be high-spirited and friendly. But there are plenty of "bad drunks" who turn nasty and even violent. Just as this chapter was being written, the news broadcasts were filled with accounts of a terrible tragedy in Europe where over thirty people were killed in a riot at a soccer match. Those on the scene report that most of the rioters were young men who had been drinking. Fortunately nothing of that magnitude has happened in the United States, but there has been plenty of violence around U.S. sporting events, so much that there has been a call to outlaw even the sale of beer at most games. Phrases like a "drunken mob" and a "drunken brawl" are not without meaning. It has been estimated that liquor has been involved to some degree in at least half the murders and assaults in the country. There are plenty of "bad drunks."

When a person is in an intoxicated state he might be moved to acts of violence that would be unthinkable in a sober state. Alcohol is one of the causes of a lot of family violence. We don't want to overdo this; a few drinks are not going to turn a normally peaceful, friendly individual into a raging monster. But if you've been to drinking parties, you know what can happen—the arguments and fights that can break out among young men boozily anxious to prove their manhood. You've seen how frustration and anger, probably tinged with drunken bravado, can lead a person to smash his hand into a wall or perhaps into someone else's face.

For most people a few drinks bring on a pleasant lowering of inhibitions, but this can be quickly followed by a loss of control. Usually the result is harmless or, at worst, embarrassing, a feeling of "Oh my God, did I do that!" the following morning. But sometimes the results can be far more serious. This is something that you should think about before you've had one too many and no longer know or care how much more you drink.

Here is one final and very important point. Evidence is beginning to accumulate that drinking during pregnancy can harm the unborn child. How great this danger may be is not yet clear, but if you are pregnant and do drink, discuss this with your doctor.

11

From the People Who Brought You Hair on Your Palms

A TERRIBLE CONFESSION

I am able to speak now. Yes, I am ready to tell you the shocking and terrible story of how I became a teenage beer guzzler. You see, from as far back as I can remember our family hid a secret from the outside world. Our front porch was spotlessly swept and shining, but guests never got past it for fear that the guests would discover the truth my family fought so hard to deny, the truth that Grandpa spiked his morning orange juice.

When I turned two, Grandpa decided it would be funny if my orange juice was spiked, too. He got a kick out of watching me stagger around the kitchen. Don't get me wrong. Gramps wasn't a bad person. He was just weird. Unfortunately, though, his good-natured prank awakened in me a deep craving for alcohol, not to mention orange juice.

By the time I was in elementary school I was a mess. I couldn't bring friends home because of Grandpa, and my friends got tired of playing on the front porch. I became a loner. What's worse I became a secret drinker, raiding garbage cans on my way home from school desperately searching for empty beer cans, madly hoping there'd be a few drops left in the can for me.

By middle school I was into bigger things. I hid a wine flask in my left sneaker. I spent my allowance money on drink. I stole money from my friends' lockers. Nothing was beyond me. There was no degradation too low for me. Soon I was flunking all my courses. My skin was blotchy, my hair oily. I looked bloated, crazed, demented. Nobody would go out with me and I couldn't blame them. I began hanging around with a bad crowd, because they were the only ones who would tolerate me.

Nothing mattered anymore except my need for alcohol. I managed to hide my terrible craving from my mother. She must have wanted to delude herself, I guess. Whenever she saw me carrying a bottle of beer upstairs and asked me what I was doing, I told her it was for washing my hair. She never bothered to ask herself why I washed my hair eighteen times a day.

Things grew even worse. I started brushing my teeth with beer. I poured beer on hamburger, used it for salad dressing, substituted it for chocolate syrup on ice cream. I began wandering the streets, forgetting who I was or where I lived. Many a time the cops found me lying in the gutter, clutching an empty six-pack and screaming for more. My breath smelled so beery the gang of criminals I hung out with drove me away from their corner.

The only thing I could do to hide the way I smelled was to hang out in front of the brewery. Sometimes a passing stranger would take pity on me and go into a supermarket and buy me a beer. Then I'd sneak off and hide behind a tree to drink it because I was afraid of being arrested for breaking the open container law.

But I would fall lower yet before I hit bottom. I threw myself at strangers, offering to go off with them for the price of a single glass of beer. They refused. I slept in the city dump just for the comfort of being near all those beer bottles. I was deranged, disgusting, disgraceful, immoral, a mockery of a human being. I deserved pity, but I was treated like dirt. Well, it was my own fault for being a wretched little wimp. Alcohol ran my life.

But I understand things better now. I've begun to pull myself up out of the mud. I don't mug beer drinkers at baseball games anymore. I don't sniff out bars. I'm going to make it. I'm going to walk tall and stand proud once more.

But I have a message for you. If you're a teenager, go to the refrigerator now and crush all the beer cans. Wear nose plugs so you will never even catch a whiff of the tainted smell of alcohol. Lecture your friends for hours on the evils of drink. Remember, it takes but one swallow to set you on the road to ruin. And in its wake will come sex, drugs, orgies, violence, and crime. You'll become so depraved you'll teach your innocent brothers and sisters to become beer guzzlers, too. So forget alcohol. Leave it to those who are older and wiser to drink themselves under the table. Bars are for grown-ups.

What you have just read is a parody of some of the "confessions" that are found in a lot of the literature on alcohol written for teens. The parody is distressingly close in style and substance to things you've probably already read. There are an awful lot of people out there who are out to try to scare you out of drinking or at the very least scare you into drinking less.

The technique is hardly a new one. It was used for over a century by temperance campaigners. One popular tract told the sensational story of how the drunkard father of a thirteen-year-old boy who had lost his leg in an industrial accident carried the leg to a surgeon and sold it for about thirty-eight cents, which allowed him to get drunk for several more days.

Aside from the terrible toll that drinking took on the individual and his family, temperance crusaders blamed it for the decline of morality and standards in general. William Goodell, a temperance crusader of the 1830s, wrote: "*Why* is *it* that sober reasoning is well nigh banished from our Senates? *Whence* these inflammatory *harangues*? *Why* is it that history and biography have lost their interest and charms? *Why are they* displaced by quixotic romance and demoralizing fiction? Why are the classic models of the last century delivered to the moles and to the bats, while the ravings of insanity are admired? Why has the inspiration of the poet degenerated into the vagaries of derangement? Lord Byron will answer. He confessed that he wrote under the influence of distilled spirits. Here the disgusting secret is developed. Authors drink and write; readers drink and admire."

Goodell either ignored or was just unaware of the fact that the drinkers of the "last century" were far more robust than the drinkers of his own time. Nostalgia has a stronger appeal to moralists than history.

Drinking was not the only practice denounced in such grandiose terms. Masturbation, for example, was presented as a grave sin by moralists and a medical disaster by many physicians who quite seriously insisted that it caused everything from madness to blindness to hair on your palms. To listen to some people today, one would think rock music will bring down Western civilization. Exaggeration and hysteria about practices that one dislikes is hardly a new phenomenon, particularly in regard to the young.

During the 1960s the hysteria focused mainly on drugs, and when it was perceived that many young people were abandoning pot for beer, it once again became commonplace to denounce drinking as threatening to the life and soul of the individual and to the moral fiber of society.

What's doubly unfortunate about the move to dust off the old prohibition arguments is that there are indeed real dangers that can be attached to drinking, but the exaggerations are not only ineffective, they may well be counterproductive. If you are given an argument that you know to be partly false, then you are likely to reject the whole argument, even though it contains many elements of truth.

Few of those who warn of the horrors of drinking today say that they are being moralistic; they contend and perhaps believe that they are simply being realistic. But they're not, and most of you know it. You can look around you and find people—lots of them—that you know, respect, and love, who drink and yet do not become hopeless alcoholics, wife beaters, child abusers, or hit-and-run drunk drivers. You read the tales of teen alcoholics and say, "That's not me," and you're right.

THE ALCOHOL SCARE

Let's take a look at some of the scariest things said about drinking and try to evaluate them honestly.

Alcohol is a drug. This is probably the most common charge, and indeed, alcohol is often called "the most dangerous drug." If a drug is defined broadly as any substance that alters feeling or mood, then alcohol most certainly is a drug. So for that matter is caffeine, but while there have been periods of moral outrage over coffee drinking these have been rare.

If one measures the number of alcoholics (no matter how that term is defined) in the country against, say, the number of heroin addicts, then alcohol is clearly the greater danger. Alcohol may indeed be more addictive than drugs like marijuana or cocaine; certainly more people are addicted to it.

But alcohol is also a drug that is woven into the very fabric of our society. Two-thirds of adults are "drug users." Drinking is part of our history and heritage. It's not going to go away. Since drinking is legal, and what is more important quite acceptable to the vast majority, the social context in which drinking takes place is vastly different from that in which other drugs are used. And that is a vital difference between alcohol and other drugs.

Alcohol is physically and psychologically destructive. The list of things that alcohol can do to your body and mind can be truly staggering. It can tear up the lining of your esophagus, cause your stomach to bleed, destroy your liver, and damage your heart. Alcohol also seems to have a permanent effect upon the brain and central nervous system. All of this and many more horrible things can happen to you after excessive and prolonged drinking. But there is no evidence that moderate drinking will do any harm at all to an otherwise normal, healthy individual. (Pregnant women may be the exception here, for we mentioned the possible harm that drinking may do to the unborn child.) Excessive and prolonged eating will make you fat and obesity carries tremendous health risks. Even stuffing yourself on a single occasion will make you sick. The problem is not drinking *per se*, but drinking too much. Indeed there is some evidence that moderate drinking may actually decrease the chance of heart attacks, and many Europeans swear that wine aids the digestion, though there is no scientific evidence for this. Many physicians feel that a drink provides healthful relaxation and is safer than a tranquilizer.

Among the great men and women of the world there have been both drinkers and abstainers.

Teens drink because of peer pressure, because they want to fit in, and because of media hype. All true, but is it a sin to do what your friends do or to want to be one of the crowd? It's very important, and it's pretty awful to feel like an outcast. Most adults who lecture about resisting peer pressures may not choose to remember just how hard that is. The very use of the word *peers* somehow makes the situation sound ominous. *Peers* sounds like some sort of alien group. Who are your peers? They're your friends, the kids you go to school with—the kids you admire and want to be admired by. Doing what others do is a normal part of growing up. Besides, you are someone else's peer—you may, in fact, be the sort of person your parents warned you against.

If you don't want to drink, but most of your friends do, that can be tough. Even if you only want to drink less than is common in your crowd, you can be under pressure. But if you are persistent, not judgmental, and merely strong about how you wish to behave, most people will respect your rights. If they don't, you would be well advised to find new friends. One rule should be, never push anyone else to take a drink.

The "media," mainly television, are currently blamed for lots of things, including alcohol abuse. Right now there is a strong campaign under way to have beer and wine ads banned from TV—hard liquor ads are already banned. Advertisers argue that their ads are not meant to increase consumption or get young people to drink, but merely to get people who already drink to switch to their brand. Such arguments strike us as nonsense. The ads are clearly aimed at promoting the image of beer and wine. The aim is to portray the drinker as sophisticated, masculine, or desirable. The image is remembered long after the brand name is forgotten. If such ads do not promote drinking in general, then they are simply not doing their job.

Whether the ads promote excessive drinking, however, is far from clear. They certainly do not promote the image of drunkenness. In any case there were drunks long before TV existed.

If you like to have a drink, there is something wrong with you. If you can't have fun without drinking, then you *do* have a drinking problem. But so often in discussions of teen drinking, one hears that kids drink because they have an unhappy home life or there are other stresses in their lives that they cannot cope with or they have not been brought up correctly or something. Certainly that figures in some teen drinking. However, the dirty little secret about drinking is that it can be fun. Even getting drunk can have a wild exhilaration about it and can bring about a feeling of near cosmic consciousness, for a time, though we hasten to add that it is rapidly followed by a sickening letdown and a hangover that makes you wish you had never gotten started. While some people become dependent upon, even addicted to, alcohol and come to hate what they drink and hate themselves for drinking, most people who drink in moderation simply enjoy it. If they didn't enjoy it, they wouldn't drink. It's no different for teens. Sure, most teens for physical and emotional reasons are more volatile and tend to get higher and lower more quickly than adults. But they still enjoy it, just as older people do.

Many who lecture teens about the evils of drinking insist that it isn't really fun or that it is some sort of fraudulent enjoyment—as compared to "healthy" enjoyment, which is alcohol-free. It is that sort of thinking that led to the dreadful and joyless workingmen's coffee houses in England that we described earlier and to some rather joyless teen coffee houses and alcohol-free parties today. The problem arises from a denial that drinking can be fun and a belief that simply being without alcohol should be stimulating enough. If the emphasis is solely on not drinking, that's no fun at all.

The American writer and humorist H. L. Mencken once defined a puritan as a person tortured by the suspicion that someone somewhere was having fun. All too often what is said about drinking and teens sounds as if it was coming from one of Mencken's puritans.

12

Summing Up

*H*ere, in abbreviated form, are some things about drinks and drinking that you should remember.

ALCOHOL

- Ethyl alcohol or drinking alcohol is the natural product of fermentation, a process which converts the starch or sugar in many grains, vegetables, and fruits (and occasionally animal products like honey and milk) into alcohol.
- Chemically pure ethyl alcohol is colorless and tasteless, though it can burn your throat like hell.
- Beer may be the most popular alcoholic beverage in the world. It is certainly the drink of choice among American teenagers.
- The basic ingredient of beer is grain. Differences in additional ingredients such as yeast or hops but primarily in the brewing process cause the difference in taste, color and alcoholic content of different beers.
- Most beer contains between 4 percent and 5 percent alcohol. While there are low alcoholic and even non-alcoholic beers or beerlike drinks, the popular light beers contain about as much alcohol as ordinary beer.

Some imported beers and the "malt liquors" have as much as 8 percent alcohol.

- Wine is fermented grape juice, but there are a huge number of different kinds of wines, and wine more than any other drink is surrounded with an elaborate ritual and lore.

- Most table wines, be they red, white or rosé, contain between 10 percent and 14 percent alcohol.

- Though chilled white wine gives the impression of being less alcoholic than red, generally it isn't.

- Fortified wines, sherry, port, and other "dessert wines" have added alcohol, and thus are between 14 percent and 18 percent alcohol. Many cheap flavored "pop" wines are fortified and highly alcoholic.

- Champagne or other sparkling wines can be produced naturally by fermentation in the bottle or artificially by injecting carbon dioxide into the beverage.

- Commercially produced "wine coolers" are mixtures of wine and some form of soda. They are usually about 5 percent alcohol.

- Hard liquor or distilled spirits can be produced from practically any kind of fermented grain, vegetable, or fruit juice that goes through the process of distillation.

- The alcoholic content of spirits are measured in proof, two proof to the percentage point. Most spirits are between 35 percent and 50 percent alcohol, that is 70 proof to 100 proof.

- Whiskey is made from grain. The differences in whiskey are due primarily to differences in the distilling or aging process.

- Vodka can be distilled from potatoes, but most vodka today is made from grain. It is colorless and nearly tasteless. Once primarily a Russian drink, its popularity is now worldwide.

- Gin is a colorless spirit. The characteristic flavor is imparted by juniper berries.
- Brandy is the name generally applied to distilled wine, though drinks called brandy are also made from apples, pears, peaches, and a variety of other fruits.
- Rum is made from sugarcane. Of all the spirits, rum's characteristic taste is closest to the product from which it was distilled.
- Liqueurs and cordials are highly flavored and very potent drinks that are traditionally taken in small quantities after a meal. They can be flavored with chocolate, mint, orange—practically anything.
- Alcohol is a food and contains some nutrients but lacks many others, and chronic heavy drinkers often suffer from vitamin deficiencies and even malnutrition.
- Alcohol contains calories, lots of them. Even the "light" beers have about a hundred calories per twelve-ounce can.

DRINKING

- America is, and always has been a drinking society. Today about two-thirds of adult Americans drink alcoholic beverages.
- When we drink, about 20 percent of the alcohol we consume is absorbed directly into the bloodstream through the stomach walls. The rest is processed at a somewhat slower rate through the gastrointestinal tract.
- Since alcohol is dissolved in the water in the blood, more alcohol will be found in those organs with a large blood supply, and the brain is well supplied with blood. Thus the expression that a drink "goes to my head" is quite accurate.

- Alcohol slows down or depresses brain activity and thus can properly be considered a drug.
- The rate at which alcohol is absorbed is affected by many things, for example, food. If you drink while eating, the alcohol will be absorbed more slowly. If you drink on an empty stomach, the alcohol will be absorbed more quickly and you will feel its effects more quickly.
- The alcohol in sparkling wines or drinks made with carbonated mixers is absorbed more quickly than straight alcohol. Water or other mixers slow down the absorption.
- As a general rule, the body can "burn off" or oxidize the alcohol in an ounce of hard liquor, a six-ounce glass of wine, or a twelve-ounce glass of beer in about one hour. That rate, however, can vary greatly from one individual to the next.
- For most people moderate drinking is a harmless, indeed pleasurable, activity. There are, however, certain individuals whose bodies do not tolerate alcohol (just as there are certain individuals whose bodies do not tolerate milk or other foods).
- There is some evidence that drinking can harm unborn children, and pregnant women are advised to be exceptionally careful about what and how much they drink.
- Even moderate amounts of alcohol when consumed with other illegal or legal drugs can be dangerous or deadly. Be *very* careful.

DRUNKENNESS

- You are drunk when you have taken in more alcohol than your body can burn off and the concentration of alcohol has caused you to lose control over your behavior.

- Whether one is drunk or not is most frequently measured by the percentage of alcohol in the blood. A person with .05 percent or below level of alcohol in the blood is generally considered sober. At .40 percent of alcohol, the drinker is almost always in a stupor, and if the blood alcohol level gets any higher, death can occur. Usually a person is incapable of drinking any more because he or she is unconscious.

- Blood alcohol levels are not a reliable guide to behavior. Some people can have their judgment severely affected with as little as .04 percent blood alcohol. Others seem able to tolerate .10 or even .15 percent and function adequately. Getting drunk is very much an individual matter. Behavior also depends a great deal on circumstances and mood.

- There is no evidence that being drunk occasionally will have long-term adverse physical effects.

- The great danger in getting drunk is having an accident. Alcohol is a contributing factor in a huge number of accidents. Auto accidents are the most numerous and well publicized, but there are also drownings, falls, and other household accidents.

- Some people become aggressive or destructive when drunk. Alcohol is a contributing factor in assaults, fights, and suicides.

- If you are drunk, black coffee and cold showers may wake you up, but they won't sober you up. You will simply be a wide-awake drunk.

- The only way to sober up is to wait until your body oxidizes the alcohol.

- There is no cure for a hangover except time.

- Coffee, hot broth, or tomato juice may help to ease the discomfort of a hangover somewhat.

ALCOHOLISM

- There is no specific test for alcoholism, nor is there even a universally agreed upon definition of the word.
- Very generally, an alcoholic is a person whose life is severely disrupted by drinking and who is unable, not merely unwilling, to stop drinking.
- Alcoholism is a disease, not a moral lapse.
- The causes of alcoholism are unknown and are probably a complex mixture of genetic and environmental factors. Indeed, alcoholism may not be a single condition at all. There may be many different types of alcoholics.
- While an alcoholic obviously drinks a great deal, sheer quantity of alcohol consumed is not an accurate measure of alcoholism. Some heavy drinkers can drink more than an alcoholic. The difference is the heavy drinker can stop, the alcoholic cannot.
- Over a period of time, heavy drinking can have serious, even fatal, effects upon an individual.
- The nature of the physical damage done by excessive alcohol and the speed at which this damage is done depend on the physical makeup of the individual and the amount that he or she drinks.
- Poor people are more likely to lose jobs or run afoul of the law because of their drinking, and they are more likely to be classed as alcoholics than wealthier people.
- While many believe alcoholism cannot be "cured," it can be controlled.
- The alcoholic does not need to "hit bottom" before his or her alcoholism can be helped. Indeed, the longer the

condition persists, the more difficult it is to control and the greater the danger of permanent physical and emotional damage.

THE LAW

- Until the mid-nineteenth century there were virtually no age restrictions on drinking in America.
- From 1920 to 1933 the manufacture and sale of all alcoholic beverages in America was illegal. Prohibition, as the ban was called, was a disastrous failure.
- During the early 1970s the age at which one could legally buy liquor was lowered to eighteen in many states. In recent years, however, the trend has been running strongly in the other direction.
- The primary reason for the move back toward higher drinking ages is the large number of alcohol-related auto accidents involving teenagers. Drunk driving may be the leading cause of death among teens.
- Adults who knowingly supply alcohol to minors may be liable to criminal penalties.
- While drunk driving was once considered a minor offense, this is no longer true, and the penalties are becoming increasingly severe.
- In some states, taverns that serve a person who is already drunk may be liable if that person later has an accident. There has been a move to broaden that law to cover the hosts at parties as well.
- History has shown that laws alone will not keep teenagers from drinking or anyone from drinking too much or driving while drunk. More important than any law is a shift in public attitudes toward responsible drinking. Ultimately the decision on whether, when and how much to drink is up to you.

13

Practical Stuff

*I*f you are concerned about drinking, either about your own drinking or the problems created by drinking in the society at large, or if you simply have been asked to do a report on some aspect of the subject, here is some information and some addresses that you should find helpful.

SADD (STUDENTS AGAINST DRIVING DRUNK)

Their motto, "Friends do not let friends drive drunk," has become a national slogan. Founded in 1981 at Wayland High School, in Wayland, Massachusetts, by the school's director of health education, Bob Anastas, SADD went national in 1982. It was the death of two of his students in automobile accidents that prompted Mr. Anastas to start SADD, and as it turned out SADD was an idea whose time had come.

SADD has chapters in thousands of high schools. There may very well be one in yours. SADD uses publicity, films, bumper stickers, buttons, and educational programs both within and outside of the classroom, as well as a variety of special projects, to get its message across. For example, SADD members promote awareness campaigns around holidays, proms, homecoming games, graduation, and even summer—the times teens tend to drink the most. It's the drinking and driving that worries SADD, not just the drinking. They help arrange transportation for teens to and from parties, encourage parents and their children to sign a mutual aid pact guaranteeing a "no questions asked for now" lift home for those who have been out drinking, and schedule alcohol-free parties and events. SADD chapters do not engage in lobbying or legislative activity.

SADD has begun a program at the junior high school level, focusing on a variety of issues including getting safe rides home for baby-sitters when their employers have been drinking. If you are interested in joining a SADD chapter at the junior high or high school level, check with your student council or guidance department. If you are interested in forming a SADD chapter or just want more information about the organization write:

> SADD
> Box 800
> Marlboro, Massachusetts 01752
> *Phone*: 617-481-3568

MADD

Mothers Against Drunk Driving was founded in 1980 by Candy Lightner, after her thirteen-year-old daughter, Cari Lightner, was killed by a drunk driver in California. The organization has a large membership and works hard lobbying for the passage of tough laws and tough penalties for drunk drivers. MADD also offers counseling services to people injured by drunk drivers.

To find out more about MADD write:
MADD
669 Airport Freeway, Suite 310
Hurst, Texas 76053

RID–USA

RID–USA (Remove Intoxicated Drivers) was started in 1978 by former New York City TV talk show host Doris Aiken when two students who went to school with her children were killed by a drunk driver. No criminal charges were filed against the driver, and this so infuriated Ms. Aiken that she established RID, which sends observers to court to monitor trials. RID, like MADD, encourages judges and district attorneys to take drunk drivers seriously and give them maximum penalties. RID makes sure judges who hand out soft sentences come to the attention of television and newspaper reporters.

To find out more about RID-USA write:
RID-USA
Box 520
Schenectady, New York 12301
Automobile Accident Victims' Hotline number: 518-372-0034.

AAIM

Alliance Against Intoxicated Motorists was formed after Carol Brierly Golin's daughter Ann, age eighteen, was killed by a nineteen-year-old drunk driver who was given a two-year-sentence in a minimum security prison and released after serving only a year. AAIM organizes "Extra

Eyes" citizen patrols to aid police in identifying and catching drunk drivers.

To find out more about AAIM write:

AAIM
Box 10716
Chicago, Illinois 60610

AA

Alcoholics Anonymous is a self-help organization providing mutual support for those who have a drinking problem. AA was started in 1935 by two alcoholics who discovered that encouraging other alcoholics to stay sober helped them stay sober, too. In the years that followed, AA burgeoned into a worldwide fellowship with thousands of chapters. Rich, poor, black, white, men, women— all kinds of people go to AA meetings, including teenagers. In some areas teens attend special meetings for young people only, as well as regular meetings.

The AA movement considers alcoholism a progressive illness, one that is spiritual and emotional as well as physical in nature. AA also believes that alcoholics can never consider themselves "cured" but can learn to get through each day one at a time without drinking. AA does not recruit and there are no dues nor are membership records kept. AA has had phenomenal success in helping people who can admit they are alcoholics and who genuinely want to stop drinking. To find out more about AA or to locate a local chapter, look up Alcoholics Anonymous in any phone book or write:

General Service Office
P.O. Box 459
Grand Central Station
New York, New York 10163

AL-ANON FAMILY GROUPS

Originally an adjunct to Alcoholics Anonymous, Al-Anon offers comfort, hope, and friendship to the families and friends of compulsive drinkers, helping them to assist the alcoholic and themselves. Al-Anon views alcoholism as a family disease, and members meet to share experiences with others who have similar problems, and to learn to reduce tensions. Al-Anon became an independent fellowship in 1954 and is a worldwide organization. The only requirement for membership is a belief that your life has been deeply affected by close contact with an alcoholic.

One of the Al-Anon groups is Alateen, for those eleven to seventeen whose lives have been affected by someone else's drinking, usually a parent. Alateen meetings are run by the members themselves, though they must have an Alanon adult sponsor. Members often go on to ACOA, Adult Children of Alcoholics. Though there are alcoholics in Al-Anon groups, those seeking help for a drinking problem should get in touch with AA.

Al-Anon publishes many booklets and pamphlets including *Alateen Talk*, a bimonthly paper. To find out more about Al-Anon or Alateen write:

Al-Anon Family Group Headquarters, Inc.
P.O. Box 182
Madison Square Station
New York, New York 10159–0182

OTHER TREATMENTS

While AA's approach to drinking problems is well known and well respected, AA is by no means the only avenue of help available to people with drinking problems. There are a huge number of doctors, psychologists, counselors, therapists, institutes, and clinics that deal primarily or exclusively with those who have drinking problems. A doctor that you know or your guidance counselor can be helpful in recommending such help. Or you can simply look in your local phone book under alcoholism, alcoholism treatment, or similar headings.

A word of caution however; in some areas anyone can call him- or herself a counselor or therapist—they need not have any special training or qualifications—and so may be an incompetent, a quack or a crook. Even individuals who are well trained can support treatments that are bizarre and useless or worse. There have also been some disturbing reports that a small number of treatment centers have been locking up patients, usually teenagers, without adequately evaluating the extent of their problems, primarily because it is financially advantageous to do so. Before placing yourself in the hands of any individual or institution for treatment, it's essential that you find out as much as you can from people you know and trust. The person who is seeking help for drinking problems is usually pretty scared and desperate and thus very vulnerable.

If you are doing a report on drinking, here are some more places to write for information:

The National Council on Alcoholism
12 West 21st Street
New York, New York 10010

National Highway Traffic Safety Administration
400 Seventh Street, S.W.
Washington, D.C. 20590

National Licensed Beverage Association
309 N. Washington Street
Alexandria, Virginia 22314

National Clearinghouse for Alcohol Information
P.O. Box 2345
Rockville, Maryland 20852

Bibliography

Englebardt, Stanley L. *Kids and Alcohol, The Deadliest Drug*. New York: Lothrop, Lee and Shepard, 1975.

Fort, Joel. *Alcohol: Our Biggest Drug Problem*. New York: McGraw-Hill, 1973.

Girouard, Mark. *Victorian Pubs*. New Haven, Conn.: Yale University Press, 1984.

Green, Shep. *The Boy Who Drank Too Much*. New York: Viking, 1978.

Hyde, Margaret O. *Alcohol, Drink or Drug?* New York: McGraw-Hill, 1974.

Langone, John. *Bombed, Buzzed, Smashed or Sober*. Boston: Little, Brown, 1976.

Lichine, Alexis. *Alexis Lichine's Encyclopedia of Wines and Spirits*. New York: Knopf, 1968.

North, Robert, and Orange, Richard. *Teenage Drinking, The #1 Drug Threat to Young People Today*. New York: Macmillan, 1980.

Rorabaugh, W. J. *The Alcoholic Republic: An American Tradition*. New York: The Oxford University Press, 1979.

Seixas, Judith, and Youcha, Geraldine. *Children of Alcoholism, A Survival Manual*. New York: Crown, 1975.

Wagner, Robin S. *Sarah T: Portrait of a Teen-Age Alcoholic*. New York: Ballantine Books, 1975.

Index

Index

Index